CHALLENGING WHITE PRIVILEGE

CHALLENGING WHITE PRIVILEGE

Critical Discourse for Social Work Education

Nocona Pewewardy

Council on Social Work Education

Alexandria, Virginia

Library of Congress Cataloging-in-Publication Data

Pewewardy, Nocona.
    Challenging White privilege : critical discourse for social work education / Nocona Pewewardy.
        p. cm.
    Includes bibliographical references and index.
    ISBN 978-0-87293-127-5 (alk. paper)
    1. Social work education--United States. 2. Racism in social services--United States. 3. Whites--Race identity--United States. I. Title.

 HV11.7.P49 2007
 361.3071'073--dc22

                                        2007008095

Printed in the United States of America on acid-free paper that meets the American National Standards Institute Z39-48 Standard.

Council on Social Work Education, Inc.
1725 Duke Street, Suite 500
Alexandria, VA 22314-3457
www.cswe.org

CONTENTS

Foreword

Challenging White Privilege: Critical Discourse for Social Work Education by Nocona Pewewardy is a courageous and important contribution to our profession's efforts to come to terms with issues of human diversity, oppression, and empowerment in relation to race. In particular, the focus on White privilege in relation to social work education addresses a pervasive feature of our profession and its implications—the numerical, political, and ideological predominance of White social workers and Euro-American perspectives. This book will challenge educators to examine their consciences about the ways that racism overtly or subtly—and always insidiously—distorts our thinking, curriculum, teaching approaches, language, and even well-intentioned efforts to promote empowerment and justice. But it also reminds us to be proud of and true to our profession's commitment to promote the well-being of all people and to work toward a society and world in which all people are honored, respected, and supported to achieve their full potential.

Pewewardy's book includes ideas, stories, and teaching suggestions that add to our profession's efforts to bring about what Rev. Martin Luther King Jr. (1992) called the beloved community, that is, a social order of care and justice for everyone. As King often pointed out, attaining that goal requires raising questions, criticisms, and actions about racism in society and our profession. This book is not conducive to complacency or lazy comfort. Rather, it promotes disquieting questions about the social construction of race, White identity, and White privilege that can spur consciousness raising and innovative actions in social work education.

Empowerment practice in social work is strongly influenced by the ideas of the Brazilian philosopher and educator Paulo Freire (Lee, 1994; Robbins, Chatterjee, & Canda, 2006). Pewewardy's book carries further into social work education Freire's emphasis on liberatory discourse that challenges taken-for-granted assumptions about social arrangements and ideologies rooted in differential privilege and opportunity. As Freire (1998) said in his final book, *Pedagogy of Freedom*: "Preconceptions of race, class, or sex offend the essence of human dignity and constitute a radical negation of democracy. How far from these values [of antidiscrimination] we are when we tolerate the impunity of those who . . . discriminate on the basis of color, burning churches where blacks pray because prayer is only white" (p. 41). Though liberatory education confronts issues difficult to face for educators, students, and the encompassing profession and society, it is filled with a sense of hope and joy arising from the conviction that things can be different and from the happiness that comes from satisfying curiosity through deep inquiry, uplifting dialogue, and the accomplishment of change. Freire said: "Hope is something shared between teachers and students. The hope that we can learn together, teach together, be curiously impatient together, produce something together, and resist together the obstacles that prevent the flowering of our joy" (p. 69). This book invites social work educators and students to move into uncomfortable spaces of oppression and complicity, hoping to find a way through into the open joy of transformative learning.

The original version of this book was a doctoral dissertation. As Pewewardy's dissertation advisor and methodologist, I was aware of the courage it took to write it. The topic itself is inherently controversial. Some students might shy away from it for fear of alienating potential employers or otherwise limiting their career opportunities. The fact that Pewewardy stuck with her idea is a testimony to her strong convictions and passion about the subject. She also creatively adapted qualitative research methodology to form a process of deep inquiry into the social construction of race, Whiteness and social privilege, and the ways these affect social work education and practice. I witnessed the way that her dissertation research was itself *discourse*. She examined discourse about White privilege by reading and critiquing literature. She also developed a way to engage prominent, experienced, and careful-thinking social work educators in a process of dialogue about their own experiences and their reactions to ideas as they developed in her unfolding dissertation. This dialogue also fed into the data analysis process to deepen and expand insights and practical suggestions for teaching. As the dissertation committee worked with her through this process, we were also part of this discourse, shaping and being shaped by the conversation. Further, Pewewardy had the courage to question herself and to grow as a person and scholar throughout all of this. This book, as both product and process of creation and application, serves as a fine example of the transformational social work education that it advocates. For these reasons, the Doctoral Dissertation Committee awarded her dissertation with honors.

In keeping with the need for reflexivity and honesty in liberatory discourse, I would like to tell some personal stories about why I am glad to support this book. I have often pondered about the ways ideas, social norms, and laws about race, Whiteness, and other classifications of people shape me and this American society. As a child, I grew up with an identity imbued by family and society as a Czech American Catholic. I had very little direct experience with People of Color until I was a young adult. Though I had a sense of ethnic and religious identity, I rarely thought of myself in racial terms, being surrounded by White people most of the time. I was sometimes prompted (and occasionally challenged by insults) to reflect on myself as a Catholic and as a member of a working-class, relatively recent generation, immigrant family. Then, in the 1960s and early 1970s, the Civil Rights and anti-Vietnam War movements challenged my own conscience about ways that I benefited, even unwittingly, from the racist and nationalistic arrangements of U.S. society. I had to think hard about what I should do about it.

When I went to South Korea to study for the first time in 1976, I suddenly found myself an obvious racial and cultural minority person. I actually enjoyed quite a bit of privilege based on that, given my educational support systems and the general goodwill of Korean people toward Americans. But the few occasions when I was laughed at, insulted, or physically threatened based on my physical appearance as a White person woke me up to a new level of awareness about power and disempowerment related to ideas about race. In particular, since I married a Korean woman who I met at that time, Hwi-Ja, we both sometimes have experienced racist reactions, because of some White people's negative opinions (or simplistic positive stereotypes) about Asians, and sometimes because of both some Koreans' and Americans' dislike of so-called miscegenation and assumptions that people who marry across race lines are traitors or at best misguided and mentally flawed. Indeed, we married just 10 years after the U.S. Supreme Court struck down antimiscegenation laws in 1967. Until then, we would not have been able to marry or have legal privileges of marriage in many states, not unlike the current situation of gay and lesbian people.

On the positive side, most Koreans and Americans have been very accepting of us as a couple. Our Korean and American families have been unconditionally accepting and supportive. I have been mentored by outstanding and wise Korean teachers and have been welcomed into sacred ways of many traditions and cultures. I have had the good fortune to witness the words and deeds of people for whom unity with diversity is not just a platitude but a way of life and action for healing and justice. My experience with all of this honed my personal objections to racism and my hope for a society and a world that reflect the ideals of the beloved community. So I am grateful for discourse that helps me and others move further toward actualizing a beloved community.

Yet, I wonder about the double-edged sword of the idea of race itself. My social work students often seem to take for granted that race is "really real." They frequently assume what they have been enculturated to believe: there are Whites (or Euro-Americans), Blacks (or African Americans), and so on, as groups with essential and distinct characteristics, typically as described in brief chapters about race or cultural diversity in survey social work textbooks, or worse yet, as defined by ethnocentric stereotypes. Sometimes the idea of race is used to oppress, as in the Jim Crow laws of the past or racial profiling of the present. Sometimes it is used to support empowerment or entitlement, such as in indigenous nations' setting of membership criteria based on so-called blood quantum, or the establishment of race/ethnic categories in affirmative action programs. Either way, these ideas about race are set in the context of the history of White racism and privilege. But is all of this really real, beyond what we make up?

My co-teacher of a cultural competency training program for child welfare workers told a funny story about how she discovered race North American style. She was an international student from a South American country. She remarked that she never knew she was Hispanic and White until she came to the United States and somebody told her! Here she quickly ran into the social and political constructions of "Hispanic" and "Whiteness" that quite surprised her. In her native country, groups were categorized with different labels and implications. Then, one time when she was visiting with a White friend, the friend suggested they go out to eat. Since this friend wanted to be sensitive to the "Hispanic's" supposed culture, she said, "Let's go to a Mexican restaurant and eat a burrito." This was a further shock, since my colleague had never thought of eating a "little donkey"—the literal meaning of *burrito* in Spanish. Although this story is relatively innocuous, of course, misuse of ideas about race and ethnicity can be at the root of all kinds of discrimination, unjustified privilege, oppression, slavery, ethnic cleansing, and genocide.

Pewewardy's book helps us think about: Who made up and who perpetuates ideas about race and Whiteness? Why do they (we) do this? Who benefits and who is harmed? How has social work been shaped by this? How does social work benefit and harm people because of this? Why do social workers so often take for granted the overrepresentation of children of color in out-of-home placements, or the supposed inevitability of disproportionate poverty, or the dominance of English in service provision, or the idea that the United States is the best and greatest nation over others, or that Euro-American-based theories of human behavior and approaches to therapy and social policy are the only ones to consider, and so on? To what extent can individuals and groups self-define themselves and choose to accept or reject conventional ideas about race, and what happens when they do? And how can White social workers challenge the pernicious effects of White privilege, and perhaps even use benefits accrued from their social station to help deconstruct White privilege itself and to advance the formation of a beloved society? This book does not raise such questions as rhetorical questions, but rather as spurs to educational action.

By extension, how can social work education promote learning processes, contexts, and relationships among students and teachers to work together in the creation of a world community in which everyone is beloved—everyone and every group is granted privilege based simply on their inherent dignity and worth? This last question represents a hope for the equal privilege of people of every color and gradation of the rainbow. Perhaps social workers can have hope, not for the erasure of privilege, but rather for the privileging of everyone together in equal, unconditional, positive regard.

Edward R. Canda
Professor and Director
PhD Program in Social Work
University of Kansas

Preface

Social workers have an ethical responsibility to pursue knowledge that supports their efforts to promote social and economic justice (National Association of Social Workers [NASW], 1999). Social work education that exposes the power dynamics underlying oppression can, however, elicit divergent opinions and stimulate emotional reactions. This is particularly true when teaching content about the intersections of racism and White privilege.

Fox (2001) noted that promoting honest talk about race and racism in a university setting can be exhausting for students and debilitating for faculty. This book is, therefore, written for educators who recognize the complexity and difficulty of teaching critical content and maintain a commitment to do it anyway. The two-part thesis of this book is that a critical perspective facilitates teaching critical content, and the contemporary discourse regarding White privilege is critical content that social work educators can use to illuminate the structural elements of racism in the United States. The following chapters provide accounts from seven social work educators of their challenges, successes, and quandaries incorporating discourse regarding White privilege into their courses.

The social work educators who participated in this study were purposively identified through their scholarship, published between 1990 and 1999, which revealed knowledge about and experience in teaching content related to the interactions between White privilege and racism. Data for the study were collected between August 2001 and September 2002. The participants provided information through two semi-structured, audio-taped telephone interviews, telephone and e-mail follow-up conversations for member checking, and an online threaded discussion using pseudonyms, which preserved their confidentiality.

Data analysis was an iterative process guided by Merriam's (1998) description of content analysis for a multiple case study design. Cursory within-case analysis corresponded with the beginning of data collection (Maxwell, 1996). The deepest findings emerged, however, from mining themes and patterns through cross-case analysis following completion of the second round of interviews. The cross-case analysis began with development of a coding guide. Data-analytic procedures were guided by Edward Canda and supported through peer debriefing with Miko Nakashima.

Discourse regarding White privilege can be a catalyst for what Freire termed *conscientization* (hooks, 1994). Conscientization is the process of "learning to perceive social, political, and economic contradictions, and to take action against oppressive elements of reality" (Freire, 1970/1997, p. 17). Freire's writings about conscientization heavily influenced the origins and the culmination of my study and figure prominently on the following pages.

My own conscientization is grounded in social work practice experiences that exposed racism as the greatest common denominator of oppression, marginalization, and exploitation. Tenets of liberatory education, such as understanding that educational systems are "created by political forces whose center of power is at a distance from the classroom" (Shor & Freire, 1987, p. 33), illuminated, for me, how discourse regarding White privilege can be a tool to counter hegemony. I found congruence in the lexicon of liberatory pedagogy and discourse regarding White privilege, particularly with use of the term *critical* as a modifier to represent power analyses. Power analyses are implied when the word critical is used as a modifier for concepts such as *perspective, content, thinking, consciousness, theory,* and *pedagogy.* These power analyses entail reflection on thought, action, and society that separates "consciousness from the dominant ideology socializing us in mass culture, daily life, and school . . . places where we internalize racism, sexism, and such values as self-doubt and love of the rich and powerful, which help wed us to the system" (Shor & Freire, 1987, p. 167).

Scholarly discourse on the topic of White privilege proliferated in the last decade of the 20th century and illuminated how racism in the United States was established through and maintained by falsely constructed notions of White supremacy (Haney Lopez, 1996; Harris, 1993; Hilliard, 1998; Kivel, 2002; Lipsitz, 1998; Thandeka, 1999). This discourse exposed how White culture in the United States is shaped by a unique set of privileges that emanated from history and resulted from genocide, slavery, exclusion, and segregation (Rains, 1998; Thandeka, 1999).

Discourse regarding White privilege also exposed contemporary benefits and advantages that correspond with racism. McIntosh (1989) likened White privilege to "an invisible weightless knapsack of special provisions, passports, codebooks, visas, clothes, tools, and blank checks" (p. 10). White people in the United States can, as beneficiaries of White privilege, expect to vote for candidates of their race, choose to receive education or job training where there are few or no people of color, and decide when and where they will respond to racism (Kivel, 2002).

Racism exists on a continuum that ranges from deadly acts of violence to subtle perceptual interactions that White privilege obfuscates. Fully understanding racism along this continuum requires mining life to figure out how it affects all people—those who are oppressed and those who are privileged as a result of their skin color (Williams, 1997). Discourse regarding White privilege is a critical dialogue that illuminates the benefits and advantages that correspond with racism all along the violent-to-subtle/perceptual continuum.

Race influences lives, even though race "is not a legitimate scientific concept that accurately describes or facilitates useful analysis of apparent differences between individuals and the groups of which they are members" (Devore & Schlesinger, 1999, p. 28). Race has no biological or scientific foundation (Christensen, 1996; Gould, 1996; Green, 1999; Smedley, 1993; Tobach & Rosoff, 1994). The meaning of race as a sociopolitical construct is, therefore, based on human interaction (Haney Lopez, 1996, 2000). Critical dialogue exposes the beliefs and behaviors that perpetuate racism and safeguard White privilege.

Shor and Freire (1987) contended that we cannot "wait for a new society before we begin transforming racism" (p. 167). Discourse regarding White privilege in the United States focuses on the history and meaning of the concept of race. It articulates the significance of race in terms of access to power and control and recommends strategies for challenging structural inequalities (Kivel, 2002; McIntyre, 1997; Wellman, 1993).

Labels such as *White people* and *People of Color* have limitations, but I couldn't discern a strategy for talking about contemporary racism in the United States without using those terms. I have, therefore, used language throughout this book that is consistent with the authors whose works informed my thinking. Tatum (1997) used the term *White* to refer to beneficiaries of White privilege. The term *White people* refers to people who are perceived as White by society, regardless of the degree to which one is aware of his or her racial identity (Kivel, 2002). The phrase People of Color is used to include the multitude of people in the United States who are targets of racism (Kivel, 2002; Tatum 1997).

The participants' wisdom and insights featured on the following pages offer guidance, inspiration, and reinforcement for social workers who are committed to liberatory education. There is a need beyond the scope of this book, however, to expand the interrogation of interactions between privileges and oppression and focus on the effects of marginalization on the basis of other intersecting identity characteristics, such as class, ethnicity, gender, sexual orientation, and ability. The complex interactions among multiple sources of privilege and oppression are introduced in some of the participants' excerpts, but these topics are not explored in depth.

Up to this point, I have referred to the seven people I interviewed as social work educators and participants. This terminology belies my appreciation for their wisdom and insights and the frequency with which our conversations reverberate through my life and inform my pedagogy. The disconnect is rectified in the next chapter where readers are introduced to the participants in a manner parallel to the way I came to know them, which was through their reflections on their experiences as evolving social work practitioners/educators.

CHAPTER 1

Introductions

This chapter introduces Mateo, Kathryn, Doc, Frances, Alicia, Rita, and Grace through portrayals that reflect how I know each person, which is through their responses to questions about including discourse regarding White privilege in social work education. Drisko (1997) suggested that providing readers with sufficient raw, qualitative data to assess the adequacy of interpretations promotes transferability, which means that readers determine for themselves the applicability of a study's findings to their setting. I have used long quotations in the following chapters to preserve the richness of the participants' descriptions and to enable readers to determine transferability to their settings.

Producing this manuscript from my dissertation research provided the opportunity to refine the participants' narratives to promote readability (Germano, 2005; Wolcott, 1994). I was, however, invested in preserving grammatical and syntactical idiosyncrasies that enlivened the participants' spoken accounts of their experiences. The following participant portrayals are ordered consistently with the sequence of the first set of interviews and reflect what I found to be characteristic of each person's standpoint.

MATEO: PASSION AND HUMILITY

My conversations with Mateo revealed an approach to teaching that was inspired by passion and tempered with humility. He described his pedagogy as being analogous to his social work practice:

> It's like social work. It's differential use of self. You as the teacher, like you as the social worker, are the instrument. You've got to know yourself and be able to work with yourself. Teaching is

1

about personal relationships for me. I don't believe in the sage on the stage imparting wisdom. I like collaborative processes, and that's something that contributes to my effectiveness. I say to students, "There's not just one source of wisdom in this room. There are seventeen sources. One of my goals is to facilitate a process that enables you to learn from each other and to realize your own sources of wisdom." I love learning myself. Each one of my courses changes every year because I've read something new or thought about something in a different way. I'm not above telling a class, "You know that stuff that I was telling you about a given topic? Well, apparently I was mistaken. There's been some new thinking about that topic. So here's the new thinking. Let's look at what I told you last week in the context of the new thinking." I don't have to be right all of the time, and I think that makes for a more effective teacher.

The following excerpt revealed how Mateo communicated to students that he sees himself engaged in an ongoing process of growth and development:

When I'm teaching a racism and oppression course I say to the class, "I don't want to give you the illusion that I'm standing up here saying I've figured out what racism is all about, and I'm no longer racist. I believe you can only be nonracist if you've lived in a society where race has never had social significance. Even if you're not a member of the Ku Klux Klan or a neo-Nazi group, it doesn't mean that you are free from racist thinking and racist ideology."

I model what I'm trying to communicate through an example that exposes how culture shapes our perceptions about gender. I tell the class, "I like feminist theory. I think that I'm a very sensitive male around issues of male privilege. But you know what? I'm still male, and I'm still socialized to be male. Every once in a while, clearly sexist notions pop up in my mind—whether I want them or not."

I've used an example from when I was flying on a small commercial jet. I'm very anxious about flying to begin with and even more on a small plane. So who gets on the plane to fly that plane? It's a woman! I described my internal dialogue, "Why do I think a man can fly this plane better than a woman?" Then I grabbed myself by the tie and yanked myself over to the corner in a joking manner as I said, "Gee, I need to have a conversation with myself." I used that as an example of sexist thinking. It pops up. I can sit around going, "Oh my God, I'm a terrible, horrible person," or I can say, "Okay, where did it come from?"

I told the class, "I was distracted the entire flight because I was examining my thoughts and ideas, and it was all an internal process. Nobody knew that it was going on, but it's still sexist." So that is an example of how I talk with my students about vigilance and attentiveness, which is what it takes to develop self-awareness and critical consciousness.

Mateo discussed his understanding of why it's hard for students to think about power and privilege:

Social workers don't want to talk about privilege, because privilege is transferred through ascription. You didn't ask for it, it comes with being male, being White, being heterosexual, having money, being able-bodied. You didn't do anything wrong. Students have to get past that notion of having done something wrong, but understand that not everybody has the same playing field. For me it's about consciousness and raising it to consciousness and being able to talk about privilege.

I might be a gay, Latino male. I can talk about being disempowered on two different levels, but I am also aware—it's like the old saying, "Thank God I was born a man." I know I get a lot of privilege from being male. I can talk about the moments in which I've been victimized as Latino and victimized as a gay man. That is true, and those experiences have been painful. But I can also talk about the moments in which I know my voice is heard simply because I'm male.

There are moments in which I've been in certain settings, and I know people are paying attention to me simply because I'm male. I was one of the founding board members of a women of color AIDS organization. I was the only male on the board. There were moments when, in discussion about different things, people would defer to me. I would say, "You all know more about this than I do."

It was the sort of unconscious granting me privilege for being male, and I made that more conscious. I would say, "This really makes me uncomfortable in that this is a women's organization run by and for women, and I am concerned that you are either consciously or unconsciously giving me a little more credit than I deserve simply because I'm a man in the room." That led to interesting conversations, because we talked about it. I declined an officer's position, and I said, "I really see my job is to support the women officers. This is part of your mission statement about you all taking charge of your life."

It's not easy. It's awkward. Sometimes I think I've got it right on the mark, and then other moments it's like, "What am I talking about?" I think I know what I'm talking about, but I [chuckles] *don't* at this moment.

Mateo's success as a social work educator materialized through the following excerpt:

When a new faculty member comes in to teach, he or she co-teach with me for a year. I'm doing it this year with one of our doctoral students who is uncertain whether he wants to teach. He's going to co-teach with me for a year.

I'm always talking to colleagues about teaching and what's effective. I make active use of my colleagues, because I don't think

I'm supposed to do this on my own. So if I have difficulty with a student, I go talk to several colleagues. I talk to a wide range of people so that I get different perspectives. When I'm flying off the handle, my colleagues can help me get refocused.

Mateo's commitment to his students was a prominent theme throughout our conversations:

The students are why I'm here. At the end of a class I always say, "You have been a gift to me, because you have taught me. You have made me grow, you have made me stretch, and you have held me accountable. You hold up for me the passion that I felt about this profession when I first joined. We can all get jaded at a moment's notice, and you won't let me. I thank you for that."

KATHRYN: AWARENESS AND ALLIANCE

My conversations with Kathryn illuminated the origins of her conscientization. She described how her investment in challenging injustice was grounded in her social work practice experiences:

I had been working with a client for an extended amount of time. She was very poor, and I didn't know it at the time, but she was living with an abusive husband—she hadn't revealed that her husband was abusive at the time of the incident I am about to describe. She had three children, and she had a child with a developmental disability. She always worked full-time or part-time, as much as she could around taking care of her children. Then her child's teacher said that he needed to start having therapy four days a week. So, she quit her job, because she didn't have a car and it was a three-hour round trip for her to get to work taking the bus. I knew that if she quit her job due to her child's disability that she would be eligible for public assistance because of the policies at that point in time. So she quit her job, and I took her in to the department to apply for Aid to Families With Dependent Children [AFDC].

I knew the AFDC worker my client was going to see. We had been working on her assertiveness, and I thought she was ready to do this on her own. I sat in the car and waited for her, and she came out and sat down in the car. When she sat down she burst into tears. After she could talk again—she was crying so hard—she said, "Some people think they can treat you bad just because they have more than you."

She had gone in, and the worker who conducted the AFDC intake, whom I knew and thought was a great person based on my previous interactions with her, had totally berated this woman because she had quit her job. The AFDC worker went off on her. So that was one instance where I thought, this has got to change. I've got to do something about this.

Kathryn described her stepwise process of conscientization:

I started by seeing sexism. I'm a White, middle-class woman, and sexism was the first thing that affected me personally so far as being a negative in my life. Obviously White privilege, heterosexual privilege, class privilege, and everything else affects me, but I didn't see that. I saw the sexism. So I began by seeing sexism when I was in high school.

Then I went to college and pursued a bachelor's degree in the area of human services. I thought that I'd be working with a lot of people who are African American, and I should know something about their culture, so my minor was in Black studies. That is when I began to see racism. Seeing racism was like seeing sexism—once you've seen it, it's there, and you can't close your eyes again. Neither of those times, by the way, had I ever heard the concept of privilege. I guess it wasn't really out there yet; this was in the 1970s.

I probably didn't have any other major changes in consciousness until I was working with a woman who identified initially as heterosexual. I really admired and respected her, and as I got to know her, she changed her identity and then self-identified as bisexual. I already knew this woman and liked her so I thought, what do I do with this? She had a major impact on me, actually, because I did already like her so much and had so much respect for who she was and what she was doing.

Then I had more one-on-one relationships with women who were lesbians and men who were gay, so at that point in time I began to see a little bit more of my heterosexual privilege. I had this major conflict in my own life about whether or not to get married and accept that privilege. I did finally get married when I began working on my PhD I decided to accept the privilege and work for change in this area.

When I was in my PhD program, I was introduced to the concept of other kinds of privileges and the intersections of oppression and privilege and identities. From there on, with a lot of mentoring at the institution where I got my doctorate, I saw one kind of thing at a time. That's why in my class on diversity and oppression we examine racism and many other sources of oppression, such as heterosexism, sexism, classism, ageism, ableism, nativism. I guess it's basically my own personal experience, looking at all of these different kinds of isms; I hope that if a student can understand one source of privilege and oppression that he or she can make the connections that will open his or her eyes to others.

The key element in my wanting to obtain a PhD was that I wanted to be able to influence a lot of social workers. I felt like there were so many gaps in my own education, particularly around working with People of Color, which was one area that really stood out for me. I felt like I hadn't been prepared as a White person to work with People of Color, and I wanted to be able to have an influence on social work education. I want students to gain some knowledge and understanding and attitudes toward social change before they begin their social work practice thinking everybody's the same and blaming the individual for their problems, whatever their problems are.

Kathryn described effective teaching as, "Getting students to look at themselves as well as others and to look at their own role in change or in blocking change." I asked her if she could think of an example of a student turning in an assignment that exemplified some kind of transformational experience.

I required my students to do something experiential for the final assignment in the diversity and oppression course. Whatever the oppressed group that they were focusing on, in addition to doing the library research, they had to do something experiential. One of the groups of students in one of my classes picked a population nearby the university that was homeless. They developed a project where they gave the people whom they met, who agreed to do it, disposable cameras to photograph their lives. Then the students gave a presentation to the class, and two of the men who took pictures asked if they could come see the presentation. I said, of course. So the two men came to the class when the students did their presentation.

It was very moving for the entire class, because it wasn't just this homeless population, kind of this anonymous group out there. Instead there were two men in the class who had participated in making the posters of their experiences and were sharing them with the students. The students in the class certainly had a transformative experience as well as the students who were in the group that completed the project.

One part of that assignment was to reflect on their thoughts and feelings as they worked on and completed their project. It was very moving when the students reflected on their experience as part of their presentation. They talked about, "These men are people to us now. We never saw them as people before. Now they're our friends. Now I walk down the street and say hi to them. I used to just ignore them like everybody else does." I was thinking, this is why I teach!

DOC: VISION AND DEDICATION

Perhaps it is Doc's social work experience as a foster care supervisor in a large metropolitan area that gave him the vision and dedication that he communicated during our conversations. One of the strongest themes that emerged early in our interviews, and continued throughout our conversations, was the connection between practice and education:

> It seems to me that when I teach about social work, I'm using my life as an example of what social work is. So the teaching is sort of an exploration of what I did as a social worker. That makes the teaching style personal. I talk about my personal professional experiences a great deal. Not in the sense of this is how to do it, but in the sense of this is what I did do. Let's see where I was useful to others, let's see where I was helpful, let's see where I screwed up, let's see where the social work profession runs into a dead end.
>
> The first time I was offered a teaching job it was at a community college. I don't speak Spanish, but my first teaching job was at the bilingual community college in the area where I live. Almost the entire student body is Spanish speaking. Many of the courses were taught in Spanish, although many were not.
>
> When I first got this job, I thought, goodness gracious, now that I've been hired as a teacher to teach this one course, what am I going to do? I started to think in terms of what my own instructors did that made me like them and what they did that turned me off. That was my first starting point. Then I came into the classroom, and I looked at the students. I know this sounds nuts, but I had no idea that everybody in class was not going to look like me.

Before I walked into the classroom I thought, "Well, OK, I'll be back at school." I went down memory lane about what my teachers were like. I thought of school as being like when I went to school as an undergraduate in the 1960s and for my master's around 1980. But there was nobody White in class, and everybody was older than I thought they were going to be. There were issues of clarity in both spoken and written English. I started to think about what all this stuff means.

Doc's stories about his classroom experiences illuminated his flexibility and fairness when interacting with his students:

I was teaching a course about four years ago or so; a student in this practice course was new to me—and new to the college, too, I think. On her midterm she got a so-so grade, which she considered bad, and she came to me and said, "What extra work can I do?" I never give extra assignments; I give out enough work for them and for me as it is. But what I do is I may give less weight to the earlier "bad" grade if the student shows marked improvement subsequently in the semester. I look at it as the getting-to-know-you process. So that's what I told her. She did great the rest of the way, and I gave her a B plus. She comes and complains that I promised if she did A-quality work the rest of the semester, she would have earned an A for the course grade. I said, "That doesn't sound like me." She said, "I don't know what it sounds like, but it is what you said."

An interesting moment. What did I tell her back then, did I promise an A? Under those circumstances it doesn't sound like me, but who knows, maybe I was tired. She sure sounds positive I did say that; who knows? So where do I go? I thought, which is more important: that I live up to my word to the student, though I can't remember giving my word, or do I maintain that I would never have made such a slip, I know myself best? I decided that it made more sense not to send a message of being an arbitrary and capricious teacher. I changed her grade to A. I taught her in several courses after that. She usually got an A, maybe a step lower, never a complaint.

In her final semester, when suddenly she was absent a couple of times (always: "I have a stomachache") or asked to leave the room to go to the ladies' room during a test ("stomach problems"), I had no problem asking what was going on. Was she pregnant, how did she know she wasn't, try a home test at least. I told her, "If you don't think you're pregnant, then let's talk about your drinking." She had no problem telling me about her boyfriend's joy at her presumed pregnancy and how now he felt she could drop out of school and he could take care of her—literally six weeks before graduation. To me, the second part of the story doesn't unfold as it did unless the first part is resolved in the way it was resolved.

ANOTHER TIME DOC DESCRIBED A BILINGUAL ROLE PLAY IN HIS CLASSROOM

Semester's great! I just came from a field seminar in which we did two great role-plays based on process recordings students did in their field placements. I have the student who did the process recording play the client, then another student play the social worker—it's an attempt to encourage students to bring case situations to class. In one case, we did the role play twice, once in Spanish. I don't speak Spanish and neither does about half the class, but it's great fun trying to assess the interview through the nonverbal communication and voice inflection, then again in English. Lots of really interesting skill and assessment issues were raised as well as some nice points about the expression of anger between a husband and wife from Puerto Rico.

I was intrigued by the idea of providing Spanish-speaking students with the opportunity to role-play in their native language, so I asked Doc what gave him the idea to do the role-play in English and in Spanish.

A couple of years ago, I had a bright student from the Dominican Republic. But, because his oral English was not developing as fast as his written, he rarely said anything in class.

I didn't want to expose him to doing a role-play in class, playing the social worker, because it seemed, I'm not sure, not quite right—all it would do is confirm the obvious, that he struggles with his verbal English. Yet I also really wanted to know, he's smart on paper, but does it translate into effective interventions? So one day in class, I set up a role-play and asked him to do it in Spanish. He was surprised but eager.

Miguel was great. I could tell by his body language that he was kind, focused, supportive, and listening actively. I designated a student as the official translator for me and the others in class. The student who did the translation gave a very nice summary, process recording style, then to my amazement provided a terrific critique of what Miguel did well and where maybe he could have done otherwise. So I wound up learning a lot about her development as well.

The more time I spent talking with Doc, the more directive I became in questioning how he had developed his commitment to social justice. In our last conversation, it came down to two very simple sentences that captured his approach to working with students: "This is complex stuff, and the only way to work towards solutions that are best for all of us is to realize that we need solutions that are best for all of us. We're all in this together."

FRANCES: CRITICAL CONSCIOUSNESS AND SOCIAL JUSTICE

The most prominent themes that emerged from my conversations with Frances are critical consciousness and social justice. Frances was unique among the participants in terms of her teaching experiences, because she left a faculty position to start her own social service agency and taught primarily at marriage and family therapy training institutes at the time of our conversations. Frances also mentored social work students through practicum placements at the agency she founded. Frances described how her ideas about critical consciousness and social transformation are often met with resistance and how she remains steadfast in her commitment to critical discourse:

> That article that you read of mine initially went to another journal. That journal rejected it saying that it was too political. I have all the edits that say it was too political. They gave me a lot of suggestions to rework it, and I refused to rework it. I got it published in a more marginal journal, because by that point I'd already had the experience of having another article rejected from a mainstream journal, and I didn't want to be in that position again. So you're talking about a journal that's supposedly more political than the rest. I mean, if you look at the editors of social work journals, look at who's on the editorial boards, they are the ones who solicit the articles, and so just by the nature and definition of who's on the editorial boards, who are the gatekeepers in those journals, they will not be open to material like this. If they take something like this, they'll want it researched in the way that the mainstream system defines as "legitimate research."

Frances discussed why she believes more social work leaders are not engaged in analyzing White privilege within the profession and in higher education:

> I don't see social work as really being progressive the way it was in its origins. Any movement, as long as it sort of nurtures a conservative flavor, will not look at political issues. It's not in the best interests of the social work leadership right now to look at White privilege. There really isn't an accreditation issue that deals with White privilege. It took many years for the accreditation structure to even require content regarding culture and gender. I don't know about your experience with that; I see even with that, with culture and gender, it's still a side course. Gender is not mainstreamed. People don't have to look at masculinity scholarship. If

they're interested in the topic, they'll look at that scholarship, but if they're not they don't have to, and they're working with families, which is why I think most female social workers have a hard time engaging men in a therapeutic process, because they haven't been taught how to do it. The question you're asking about White privilege is really isomorphic to the way content is being integrated around culture and gender.

I asked Frances what inspired her commitment to stay connected to social work given some of the conservative influences she described:

I think that commitment comes from the fact that I see social work as being the place where a lot of great things can happen. I mean, when you compare it to family therapy or even psychology, it is so much broader, it really has in its origin a systemic base. It's unfortunate that the clinicians who have come through social work education went into all kinds of different schools of thought, like the cognitive school and whatever, and lost the systemic way of informing practice.

I think that there are more social workers treating our families than anybody else, so there's a real basic survival issue. I don't think that I can leave what I have to offer and go even just into family therapy, because I think that the majority of people providing practice, providing services in this country, are clinical and social workers. If there's any hope in terms of changing social service delivery, that's where it has to happen.

I think social work holds a broader conceptual possibility, as compared to family therapy that tends to be systemic, but still tends to be defined as family therapy rather than policy. So it comes from that place where I think social work was and where I don't think it is today. I mean, I have chosen not to take a university position just because I couldn't live in academia today. I still identify as a social worker/family therapist because I think it provides people with the leadership that they don't have. When I present, even at the National Association of Social Workers (NASW), people come up to me and say they're so proud to know that I'm a social worker, because they don't think that social workers like me exist. So that feels good that people are willing to look at other perspectives, and I feel like in a very tiny way, if I can begin to influence people, that there is another way to do this.

Themes of critical consciousness and social justice were reflected in Frances's response to a question about how she would describe the goal of her teaching:

The goal of the teaching is to have people develop the critical consciousness to understand that we have choices, that people have choices and that the particular position one's born into or one's life choices are not permanent, it doesn't have to be static. Consciousness really is a choice, so that people can really be helped to move and get a better understanding of what needs to happen to have a sort of more balanced view of race, gender, class, and all of the other intersectionalities.

I was encouraged when Frances described some of the benefits of her perseverance:

I guess the only thing that I feel has always worked for me, both in the organizations that I've worked with and the way I've really moved my own organization from a place where I had a lot of challenges by the White structures, is that I formed coalitions with People of Color and with White people who understood the political narrative. I kept going regardless of what the White institution said, to the point now where people are coming to us, because they realize the power base we have.

ALICIA: REFLECTION AND SENSITIVITY

The characteristics of reflexivity and sensitivity emerged during my conversations with Alicia when she described her love for teaching:

At one point I realized I think of it as a spiritual activity from the point of view that I see spirituality as having to do with meaning making, understanding, interpreting, comprehending. I'm left feeling that I'm privileged to have ended up in teaching and challenged by learning how to teach better as I participate in peoples' intellectual and emotional development.

I asked Alicia how her view of teaching as being a spiritual experience influenced her interaction with her students:

I really appreciate your framing it in a positive perspective, and thinking about how to attract faculty to do this, because over the years, learning how to teach and teaching the diversity content, in particular, has had its painful moments. Yet, I can't think of any moments that were not growth promoting. For example, like screening videos before I show them in class. The second example is, in fact one of the presentations I made on the article that you and I talked about the last time, where at a national presentation, I read an excerpt from one of the participants and I was moved to tears. I had to stop and take a deep breath to continue. I was just so moved. So when I say it's difficult, that's the kind of thing I'm referring to, these emotional jolts that to teach social justice one has to deal with and not be put off by.

Alicia had explicitly talked about White privilege in the scholarship that I used to identify her as a participant for this study. When I asked her where those ideas came from, she described a period in the 1970s that was influential in her development:

I had a period between 1970 and 1977 where I was a psychotherapist at a university after getting my master's in the late 1960s. This was during the Vietnam War, and I think everyone in that period was very aware and wanted to do something, and wanted to know what the right thing to do was. I did a lot of reading on social inequality from a leftist perspective in terms of socioeconomic class and self-interests of different classes. I look back and see that as a period where I was politicized.

I went through a lot of changes during that time, but a couple of things stood out for me. One was that I realized that for me to be an effective clinician in that university setting, students needed to know where I stood politically, that I couldn't be a vague, ambiguous clinician. I had to be clear about where I stood. It was expected in that environment. Students trusted me when they knew what my beliefs were and where I stood on some of the political issues.

There were many demonstrations at that time. I became aware of realities that come out of what feminists call standpoint theory. Standpoint theory addresses how what we perceive is filtered through our life experience and privilege and resources or lack of those in our lives. So with those assumptions, I saw things a lot differently. For me, that was the basis of beginning to write and publish. I found myself noticing more of the sociopolitical influences in society. Consumerism, for instance, is an example of what we're socialized into by virtue of capitalist cultural and economic influences. Those ideas must have resonated with some of my experience as a young adult in terms of explaining my experiences.

It's interesting that you asked about that, because that was such a powerful experience for me in the 1970s that even now, with the writing, I'm doing I find myself going back to some of those principles and concepts about class conflict and power issues. These have an important place in understanding behavior and self-concept and understanding oppression. I try to focus on ways that people can get a handle on them to change their lives, to make their lives more manageable, and on the implications for practice.

Alicia also described how her experiences in the 1970s influenced her approach to teaching:

That period I was talking about, in the 1970s, was so influential for me. The main learning that I gained during that period has stayed with me—particularly with regard to understanding that the dynamics of oppression are socioeconomic and political in nature, rather than exclusively psychological. I find the real challenge for micro practitioners is to be skilled at the micro level and to practice in the context of the larger sociopolitical picture.

Alicia described how her practice differed from more conventional approaches to clinical social work:

My area is mental health. The last clinic I worked in had a multinational Latino staff, including a clinical psychologist. My first point is that it depends on who the clinicians are, because we were a very good team, particularly from the point of view of looking at the person in context—the culture and socioeconomic class. I included a wide range of factors in formulating problem areas and in prioritizing those areas in someone's presenting problem. This summer I went to a workshop on Bowen theory, and there was some discussion about how systems theory needed to be applied more to individual behavior. I was a little surprised to learn that view wasn't a basic assumption, but it reminded me that probably practitioners often view behavior from a narrow perspective. They often only look at factors that are within the person, i.e., psychological, such as conflicts, limitations, and ego functions.

From my point of view, with the origins of social work in settlement houses and identification with the disenfranchised, I assume that in becoming knowledgeable about vulnerable populations and providing services that our work involves advocacy. It's a major part of the social work professional identity. That applies to the most clinical of roles, where you're doing psychotherapy, the social work values with that history, involve looking at behavior in context. When there are social justice and oppression issues in the client's life, it is important to probe in those areas. I use that as an example because clinical social work is often seen as only individually focused.

There's also the issue related to our role in raising social justice issues. I think we need to keep an ear open for social justice issues from the point of view of looking at behavior in context. I see social justice as built into social work practice. Likewise, oppression is central from the point of view of looking at behavior in context. When we provide services to individuals, some of the change will be with the clients and some of the change effect will be with the agencies and institutions. I see it as essential that clients have some understanding of societal values and beliefs that shape their sense of self.

Alicia's reflection, sensitivity, and ongoing learning came through when she described a significant relationship with a colleague:

There is one friendship that stands out that I have with one of my colleagues who has been disabled all of his life, and he's in a wheelchair. One of the things I've learned through my relationship with him, that I will bring up in class, is how ableist our language is. I think the first time I noticed was when I said to him, when I was feeling overwhelmed, something about feeling I couldn't walk and chew gum at the same time. Then he and I laughed about it—and he said, "He couldn't roll and chew gum at the same time." More recently, it's that friendship that has really opened my eyes from the point of view of a person with a disability. So that has been tremendous learning and growth for me.

Alicia described her developmental process as an educator as being one of "finding balance between the content and the process."

RITA: PERSPECTIVE AND HOPE

Information about Rita's development as a social work educator surfaced through her discussion of her approach to teaching:

For me, this is very much an evolutionary process. I started out primarily as a teacher of clinical practice and had my hands full doing that. I chaired the clinical practice department. I directed the doctoral program for a while. I've written about a number of things along the way. But I think the route that got me most interested in this topic was that I've always been interested in community. Even long before I ever knew there was a profession of social work, I was raised in a Christian context that really exposed me to the Bible in a very detailed way. I saw Jesus as a social radical. I didn't know any of this language at that time. I was just impressed with things, like the rich man has as much difficulty going to heaven as the camel through a needle's eye, and statements about Jesus and his concern for people who were poor and marginalized.

Then I started college and found it possible to meet really radical people who were affiliating that with their Christian Protestant commitment. By that point I guess I was pretty radicalized, and I was torn in two directions because the place that I got money to go to graduate school for my master's was a highly psychodynamically oriented and individually and intrapsychically oriented program. So here I was, on the one hand sort of being a social radical and doing community organizing and working with people who were working in poor communities and involved with student nonviolence initiatives and all sorts of things like that. Then on the other hand I was learning this tremendously individualistic, intrapsychically oriented perspective on practice. My short-term resolution of that was to get involved in community mental health. In those days, which were the late 1960s and the early to mid-1970s, the community mental health system I was working in was really very progressive. It was an exciting place to be.

Then I got my doctorate at a program that promoted ecological ways of thinking and continued musing about the idea of community, which had always been the bridging point for these two perspectives for me. Sometime in the last three or four years, I'm trying to remember just exactly how the transition from community to social justice happened, I began thinking more and more about communities and exclusion and the people who didn't get a chance to participate in community and so forth.

Rita talked about how her pedagogy and scholarship is informed by critical analyses:

I think that what has happened is that I have been increasingly critiquing everything from a social justice perspective, and in some ways it's kind of a long reach when you think of where traditional practice theory, particularly individual and family practice theory, has evolved and where it came from and so forth.

I had a doctoral student who was in a class, and one day I said something like, "I think it's really clear for people how social justice relates to larger-scale kinds of practice, but I don't think we've really begun to adequately explore how ideas of social justice relate to direct practice and that there's a great deal more there to do." You could see this was one of those electrifying moments for this student. Then a couple of weeks later she said to me, "I went and asked my students what they thought about this. I actually had them write it down. It was so amazing because some of them really could make a very direct connection while others were clueless." Then she and I started talking about teaching and in what kinds of ways we could much more directly teach this content. Now that follows the article that you cited in your letter of introduction.

That article really came about from faculty processing around issues of racism. Within the faculty, beginning to articulate the idea that there was such a thing as White privilege and that White racism was a different kind of racism than other kinds of racism. Yes, you could be biased or prejudiced, or maybe you could even call it racist if you were members of other groups, but the power resided with Whites and so White racism had all kinds of structural and institutional effects.

One of the things that I will have to say in credit to the faculty where I teach is that it's a faculty who are very open to learning. We have done a lot of professional development with regard to understanding intersecting oppressions and exclusions. We've processed material that promoted a deeper understanding of issues faced by gay men and women. We've focused on the topic of racism in our staff development efforts. In the midst of that process, we remarked upon the fact that most of the faculty had been educated in an era when there weren't courses on racism. So here was this interesting paradox. We've tried to have the racism and oppression courses taught by a broad cross-section of faculty— part-time and full-time, faculty of color and White faculty—and to have a mentoring process so people who teach that course observe it first and have somebody to talk to.

In the second interview Rita described the impact courses on racism and oppression have had on the faculty and students at her institution:

I think racial identity theory has been very helpful in the sense that it provides a contextual way of understanding oneself, whether you're a White folk or a Person of Color. So the faculty here have learned from that, and the students read it and learn from it. We have a strong developmental emphasis in the program, in a whole variety of ways, including self-development. We've all sort of grown and gotten more sophisticated in how to address these issues in constructive ways.

In spite of the fact that there was an enormous amount of distress on the parts of students 10, 15 years ago about the course on racism and oppression, these days the students love it, and there isn't the stress about it. They really feel that it's terribly important. If anything, they get upset that we don't do a better job of incorporating this content into other courses. I think the course is working very well.

But we must remember that change is incremental, and we have to have some degree of comfort with the slowness of the process sometimes and just keep working at that. We have to be able to engage in critical and compassionate self-reflection. I think that oftentimes we take one of two approaches to being critical. One approach is to search into the core or political. Another way of being critical is to be disparaging. It is important to find ways to approach critical thinking with compassion in order to sustain oneself and support each other through this hard work.

When I was talking with Rita, I sensed that the institution where she teaches is in a more progressive developmental stage than the social work profession as a whole. This was supported to some degree when Rita described the editorial reviews that she received on an article she collaborated on with one of her doctoral students:

I eventually wrote a paper with the student I was talking about before about our experiences teaching social justice content, and it is languishing in the process. It has been rejected by one journal, and I thought that their objections were bizarre. I say that as a person who is multipublished and also an editor for a major social work journal.

The article was rejected for lacking a sufficient theoretical foundation. I was particularly irked about this because the article was about teaching. The article wasn't a philosophical treatise on what do we mean by social justice. Since we were talking about how you teach about social justice, I felt the review was a bit hair-splitting.

Rita's description of having an article about her experiences teaching social justice content rejected for lacking an adequate theoretical foundation reminded me of Frances's discussion of having an article rejected on the basis that it "was too political." This was a catalyst for asking Rita a question about how much discourse regarding White privilege she finds in social work:

> Within social work we sometimes do better about this than at other times. I think that we've probably done a lot better about multiculturalism than we have about White privilege. That basically says it's easier to look at other people than to look at ourselves, given that most social workers are White. We continue to need to work on that.

GRACE: WISDOM AND COMPASSION

One of the main themes that emerged across the first set of interviews was that the seven people I talked to seemed to be able to work effectively with students at various stages of development. I discussed this idea with Grace early in our second interview, and it was during this phase of our conversations that I came to think of her as the personification of wisdom and compassion. Evidence of Grace's wisdom and compassion emerged from her reflections on some of the influences that bring students into social work education and how she tries to empower students to work for social justice:

> A lot of our students pursue social work because they're idealistic and compassionate and want to make things better. What is important to stress with people is that we all have our own comfort zones, and if you try to step out of your comfort zone and you're not ready to, the outcome could possibly not be good—so to really help people see they need to honor their comfort zones. An example I give is a woman I know who had never been in a protest march, and the first time she decided that she needed to join in this group and go on a march, she hid behind the sign the whole way so nobody would recognize her.
>
> For some people wearing a button that says "Stop Racism" is no big deal. They just wear the button. For other people to wear a button like that is to feel like they're walking around totally exposed and vulnerable.

I try to give students examples of how one person's comfort zone is different from another person's, and you have to honor your own process. You never jump from *A* to *Z* or *A* to *M*. You go *A, B, C, D*, in terms of your life's journey. If we do jump too far ahead of ourselves, and we're not ready for it, we're not only going to compromise what we can learn from the situation, but it could backfire on us. I talk to students about going just far enough out of your comfort zone that you know you can handle it. You're scared, but it's not so overwhelming that you can't handle it. That's pretty much what I did early in my own career. Each time I was presented with the next thing to do, I had to say, "Can I do this?"

I also tell the students never to minimize small actions—no action is too small and no retreat is irreversible. Somebody may tell a racist joke, and you don't say anything one time. You go home and you feel horrible about it, you struggle with it, you can make up for that. It's not the ultimate failure. If they just stay with taking care of themselves but doing the next right thing as they understand it in that moment and are continually in process, even though it can be scary, it doesn't have to be immobilizing and everything can work out.

I try to give examples of role models. Like Rosa Parks didn't wake up one day and say, "I think I'm not going to give up my seat today." She went through a very long process of very mundane things that she did before that moment came. I guess it's about helping students be right-sized and take it one step at a time.

Grace described the way she developed her understanding about White privilege:

I'm still in process, and I've been teaching this stuff for years—I think a dozen years. I'm still in process, so I don't expect people to get it in a class. It's just another step in their journey. So for me personally, I started at quite a young age identifying with the oppressed but never getting it that I was in any way connected with oppression. I always saw myself as taking up for the "underdog"—always taking sides with people who were getting the short end of the stick.

In the 1960s I got involved with the Civil Rights movement with Martin Luther King Jr. because I was incensed about the injustice and a bit self-righteous that I was different from other White people. It's another stage that I see the students going through that I'm not like the rest of them; I care and I've been working for social justice. I got involved in consciousness-raising groups about women's issues and started to get that it might have something to do with my own social identity as female.

I look at how my consciousness evolved. It started with externalizing and looking at other people rather than looking at myself. I developed the understanding that some people are getting the short end of the stick, and there are certain predictions you could make about who is going to get the short end and who is not. Then it got closer to home when I looked at my position as a female, but even then there was a lot of denial that I had experienced any oppression. I had to dig for it because I'd internalized so much. Then, the last step for me was getting at my Whiteness and Beverly Tatum and Ruth Frankenberg—I thought their stuff was fascinating. Their work pushed me into looking at how I feel about my Whiteness and acknowledging that Whiteness is a social identity. Now, instead of calling myself Caucasian or European American, I acknowledge that I'm White, and that is a culture in and of itself in the United States. So I guess reading, self-reflection, journaling, teaching this class for the last dozen years, and doing research and writing and immersing myself in critical discourse has really been a part of my own personal journey.

The need for educators to understand how privilege and oppression operate in their own lives, before they attempt to teach this type of content, was a strong theme during my conversations with Grace:

The first thing that comes to mind is that phrase, "Physician, heal thyself." I think one of the most important things that it seems you're getting at is what are educators' personal experiences and what do we need to do in order to teach this? There's an old joke, "Those who can do. Those who can't teach." That doesn't work. I think that if we're going to teach about this effectively, we have to be able to do our own work in understanding these issues.

I often jokingly say, "There are two kinds of people in social activism," but I think it's true in terms of faculty and true with our students. There are people who really want to change the world for the better and want to be part of that change, and there are people who really want to be a little bit better than everybody else [laughter]. I've gotten good at spotting where people are at in their developmental process in that regard, and I'm beginning to think that there needs to be sort of a self-righteous stage. It fits with the stages of racial identity development, too, that there's kind of a self-righteous stage where you gain some insight, and you want to show everybody else that this is the way to go. I see that there's some faculty who are at that stage, and they get very frustrated with students, and I've been at that stage as a faculty member. I can revert to that stage when I get impatient or when I've got a particularly resistant student. I can really want to hammer people over the head and scream, "Why don't they get it?"—as if I do [laugh]. So I have my moments.

I think that the people who really immerse themselves in teaching about power, privilege, social justice, and diversity issues either will burn out if they don't continue to grow and learn from the experience or they get very angry and don't want to teach social justice content any more or they just become very ineffective. People who don't teach discrete courses on diversity and oppression—where you're really in there sink or swim—don't have to do the same level of struggling. Or maybe they do the struggling at a different place.

SUMMARY

In describing their professional development and approaches to teaching, Mateo, Kathryn, Doc, Frances, Alicia, Rita, and Grace reinforced the notions that a critical perspective facilitates teaching critical content and that the contemporary discourse regarding White privilege is critical content that social work educators can use to illuminate the structural elements of racism in the United States. All of the participants described a process through which they developed their current perspectives about the structural nature of White privilege and racism. Their willingness to share their experiences with students as a way to model the development of a critical standpoint reflected engaged pedagogy and illuminated a strategy for empowering students to evaluate their own values, attitudes, and beliefs.

Teaching critical content is a challenging endeavor because an educator can never fully predict how students will respond to material that challenges the narratives on which they may have built their hopes and dreams (e.g., the myth of meritocracy). Using material in the classroom that has the power to arouse consciousness can stir emotions. Flexibility and a willingness to improvise helps educators start where students are (Fox, 2001), which is analogous to the principle in social work of starting where the client is.

Every social work student is an individual with a unique threshold for discomfort, and each person must go through many steps in his or her process of growth and development. Part of effective social work education involves mentoring students through aspects of their developmental progression. This requires instructors who can engage with students through a collaborative process of mutual shaping and reciprocal learning. Discourse regarding White privilege is a resource social work educators can use to increase their own critical awareness and introduce students to the structural nature of racism in the United States.

CHAPTER 2

The Potential of Discourse Regarding White Privilege as a Catalyst for Transformational Critical Consciousness

The participants revealed information about their consciousness that illuminated why they had looked behind the veil of racism to find its functions and beneficiaries. Discourse regarding White privilege in the United States derives from analyses of interactions among power, privilege, and oppression (Haney Lopez, 1996; Hurtado, 1996; Lipsitz, 1998; Pharr, 1996). The participants arrived at discourse regarding White privilege through critical analyses of the antecedents of social inequalities and used this content in their courses to engage students in thoughtful dialogue about the structural nature of racism and other forms of oppression.

Figure 1 provides a visual representation of consistencies in the participants' conscientization process that emerged through inductive, cross-case analyses of their data. Each person discussed how his or her awareness of White privilege evolved and evidenced critical thinking that would result in ongoing growth and development. I termed what emerged about the participants' similarities in process and standpoint *transformational critical consciousness*. Commonalities among perpetually interacting elements of transformational critical consciousness also surfaced. These elements included *development, application, regeneration, conscientization*, and *academic synergy*.

A corollary relationship between the participants' consciousness and discourse regarding White privilege materialized from their narratives. Each participant's standpoint was grounded in transformational critical consciousness that emanated from structural analyses of interactions between privilege and oppression that were inspired by a commitment to social justice. Flynn's (1994) articulation of social justice, which focused on equity, equality, and fairness in the distribution of societal resources and placed an explicit value on achieving social equity through democratic processes, resonated with the participants' use of that term. It is, therefore, Flynn's definition of social justice that is implied through use of that term in the following chapters.

FIGURE 1: Transformational Critical Consciousness

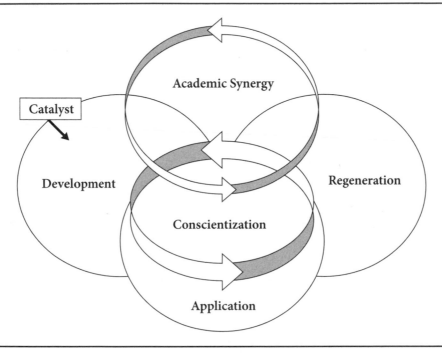

CATALYSTS AND DEVELOPMENT: INKLINGS THAT SPARK CRITICAL ANALYSES

Transformational critical consciousness is a personal paradigm shift that begins when a person detects incongruence between his or her sense of justice and the norms and values that pervade social arrangements. Development of transformational critical consciousness results from catalysts that illuminate discrepancies between a person's expectations and his or her experiences.

All of the participants identified catalysts. Some catalysts were grounded in early social work practice experiences, which was the case for Doc:

> When I graduated from college, I didn't know what to do. Somebody said, "Hey, why don't you get a job working for the Welfare Department?" So I got the welfare job. In those days the welfare worker was responsible for a caseload of between 60 and 75 families. You had to make visits four times year, and you had to

figure out budgets and all that kind of stuff. It was case management plus financial determinations. I was pretty good at it. I was pretty good at it because I'm smart enough to figure out how to do forms and follow procedures, and I had enough of a heart. I cared enough about the lives of the people I was working with. I had never encountered poverty until I did this job. I certainly didn't come from a well-off or even middle-class background, but I never saw poverty and the effect of racism until I encountered it on this job.

Doc's description of his early practice experiences, combined with how he currently thinks about race, illuminated an evolutionary quality of development:

There's no silver spoon in my mouth. But I still have White privilege. In Chris Rock's HBO special, he says, "The White maintenance man of this theater would never trade places with me. And I'm rich." Indeed, I may have come from a lowerish-class background, with all sorts of financial problems and my own family's wacky dynamics, but still, when I walk into family court, nobody assumes that I'm the client. *Nobody* assumes I'm the client. They always assume I'm the social worker.

Grace located the catalysts for her development in her early career and talked about the evolution of her determination to work for structural changes:

I started out as a teacher in the late 1960s, teaching high school English, and I immediately went through a kind of shock. If you've read any of Jonathan Kozol's books where he described schools in poor communities and how bad they are—well, I was immersed in one of those types of schools, and I think I was 20 years old. I had just graduated from college, and that was my first exposure to the inequities and injustice of the system.

I had a lot of passion, a lot of feelings of passion. I was angry about the injustice. I was determined to change the system. I was young. I had a bit of an inflated idea of what kind of a change I could bring about, which is probably good, because it really got me in there doing things and taking risks that I wouldn't have taken otherwise. I was very upset about the inequities, and it threw me into a lot of inner turmoil, a lot of conflict about how I was raised and anger that nobody had told me as I was growing up that this is what the world was like. I had a lot of compassion, particularly for the kids I was teaching.

I think my commitment to social work is just as strong now as it was then. But I feel much more humble now than I did then about a lot of things. The first thing that comes to mind is about how much one person can actually do. When I started teaching in the late 1960s, I was young and pretty self-righteous and a little arrogant. Although people wouldn't have characterized me that way, that's really how I tended to feel—you know, "I'm just a cut above those poor peons who don't get it, who don't care." That's totally changed now. Now I realize more and more how much I don't get it, how I need to make informed decisions about what's the most effective, not just what will make me feel good.

The biggest thing that has changed in my life is that I am now the power. That is probably more uncomfortable than any other position I've ever been in. It was a lot easier to be 25 years old and not care about job security and not be in a power position to run off and do things. Although I did struggle, because I did want to sell out and probably did sell out some times. I just don't remember those times [laugh].

Rita evidenced how academic discourse can be a catalyst:

I grew up universalizing the color-blind world. This was before multiculturalism, when everything was unquestioned, and Whites were likely to say they were color-blind and didn't appreciate that was pretty insulting to People of Color because it discounted the real effects of racism. I think the ideas you are referring to in my scholarship grew out of faculty in-service trainings around racism. We probably read the McIntosh article in the midst of that and read other stuff and had some speakers and some workshops and some things like that.

This discourse illuminated that it's not just a question of there are us kind of average blokes, and then there are folks who are oppressed. There's actually unearned privilege that's being taken advantage of all the time. I think talking about White privilege is tremendously illuminating.

I guess the other thing that I want to say somewhere in here is that I think somehow or other we have to find ways of talking about privilege so that people don't end up feeling totally guilty and ashamed and immobilized. That's where thinking about discourses, some of the framings that come from the narrative perspective that really identify how all people are impacted by cultural understanding, can be useful because you can take responsibility for change without having to feel like it's your own crummy fault that you got into this in the first place. So helping everybody analyze the sort of social or cultural discourses that perpetuate a whole series of things, such as "that we really do deserve it" or "there is a level playing field." We could go on listing lots of cultural myths about why things are the way they are and that take people in power off the hook and make them look righteous.

APPLICATION: ARTICULATING BELIEFS THROUGH BEHAVIOR

Application embodies consistency between a person's evolving consciousness and his or her behaviors. While the concept of development represents the incubation of critical analyses of structural inequities, application reflects making those analyses explicit and engaging in behavior that challenges oppressive elements of the status quo. All of the participants described how critical analyses of racism revealed White privilege. Kathryn described how understanding the correlation between White privilege and racism influenced her approach to social work education:

> The whole thing comes down to access to power, and if Whites did not have more access to power, then racism, which is having less access to power, could not exist. That's an assumption that I accept, that White privilege is very real. Including I have it. I'm White, and I assume that White privilege is very real, and that underlies everything I teach. Anything. When I'm talking about class issues or any kind of social justice issues—that's part of my lens for seeing the world—is to assume that White privilege is real.

Mateo's critical analyses exposed the association between White privilege and power:

> If you have privilege, you have power. The way I look at privilege is, for a lot of people, it is unconscious power. If you are educated, for example, you use education as a way of changing your class status. I think people do realize they have acquired access to new power by earning a degree. "I will get more money, I will get more status, I will get this, this, and this." But privilege, when we're talking about privilege in terms of race or gender, it's often unconscious.
>
> What I think is uncomfortable for a lot of people is when it's brought to consciousness, and then they realize how much real power they have. What does it mean to have White skin? What doors are opened, what assumptions get made? What assumptions get made if you're male or you're female? When people become clearer about privilege and understanding it, they become clearer about power. Power is an issue that social workers have a lot of trouble talking about, because I think most of us are aware of the abuses of power.
>
> Most of us can't get through life without being in a situation where we've been abused by somebody who's had more power than we have. The resulting notion, because we've experienced

people who've abused power, is that power is bad. But it's not. We all want power. All of us do. We want to feel effective. We want to know that we have an impact. It's getting people to realize that power in and of itself is not a good thing or a bad thing. It's how you use the power you have. If you are unwilling to consciously think about power, you will probably abuse people with your power because you haven't thought about the fact that you do have power. For example, you might feel as a White, female social worker that you don't have a whole lot of power. Be a mother who receives public assistance. Her perception is that you have *all* the power.

Doc demonstrated application through a description of introducing the concept of privilege in his social work courses:

First of all, you have to identify the issue. The first thing is to identify White privilege and then to talk about where it rears its head, and that's everywhere. That includes the dynamics of supervision. It includes the dynamics of how agencies are organized and how you work for change inside of an agency—to get it into my policy class. It's the introduction of themes, clarification of what it is you're trying to talk about, and then devising exercises that allow students to explore it. And above all, provide an atmosphere where that exploration can be done as safely as possible—where people feel safe to say to me, "Hey, you're a White guy, too." I say, "I am, so go ahead with the discussion."

Kathryn, Mateo, and Doc focused on the importance of explicating White privilege. Frances revealed how White privilege can influence students' educational experiences and what she has done to contest privilege:

I want to say something about this whole concept of mentorship, because I think that there's a real skew around mentorship. In the family therapy field there's been this idea of mentoring where a lot of the White people will mentor People of Color as a way of bringing diversity into the whole organization. But what has happened is that a lot of White senior therapists have actually exploited the minds of younger therapists of color. They have mined information from their protégés, have coauthored articles, but they've been the first author. It's colonization under this disguise of actually mentoring and creating visibility.

What this does is co-opt knowledge, and it maintains the authority of the first-world person. We've had that conversation, and it hasn't gone well, because people who are doing the colonizing don't want to think of themselves as colonizers, especially liberal Whites. They want to think of themselves as being just. But we have raised the question in many forums about, "What it would look like if you were to mentor somebody and actually, in the process of mentoring, have them be the first author. What would that look like?"

There are some younger White people who are really very open to these ideas and really see it. The more privileged and the more established the White people are, they find a way to get around it and not deal with it. We've got to be very careful about where we have these conversations, but it is a real issue of how that whole notion of mentorship can benefit the mentor under the guise of publishing or publicizing a certain experience of oppression.

The other thing that's happening a lot, which is really bothersome, is a lot of people now are going overseas to teach in Africa and Australia. A lot of very well-known family therapists, and I say to myself, "Why would they go and not take a Person of Color with them? What is that process that they feel entitled to go and take their knowledge to the African continent without any conscience or embarrassment?" I don't think they even consider that. It's just that they've been invited, and they see themselves as offering some knowledge, and who they are as bearers of that knowledge gets completely obscured.

Frances also described contesting privilege when it resulted in low academic expectations for a student of color when diversity was uncritically confounded with oppression:

I found the White faculty to be almost not having any standards for many students who are racially different. It's almost as if they overaccommodated. That's the other side of racism where there's virtually no expectations. That's one of the conflict areas I had, because I'm willing to work with students, but I also have a high standard of what I expect them to do.

For example, there was one student in particular who comes to mind a few years ago. He was Latino, he's gay, and he's a man, of course. He had gotten through most of his life and also in the first year of graduate school by being very charming and not really doing what he had to do. He always had the excuses of how he had to take his parents different places, he couldn't be there on the number of days, so when we first started the placement he renegotiated immediately the first week that he could only be there two long days instead of three days. We tried to negotiate that, worked it out, and then he was supposed to be running some joint activities for the kids. It was a school placement with one of the younger women social workers. He managed to leave early the second night as well, so I challenged him on it, and he went to his advisor and his advisor said to me, "He's having a really hard time." I said, "If he's having a hard time then he needs to drop out. We can consider a different placement but we can't keep cutting back what he's expected to do. There are three other students in this placement, and I don't think it's fair. Besides which, he's really not even doing the minimum amount of work he has to do to get through."

They put him in another field placement where he had similar troubles. He ended up getting through, but still had to do a whole lot of extra hours, so he came back into the field placement with me, and when he came back to me he basically said he came back because he felt that he wasn't learning anything at all in the other placement. He conveyed that it was easy to get through, but he wasn't learning anything. We had a long discussion after that about what it means to be male and have male privilege and to be a Person of Color for whom people have low expectations. Because he was male and there were very few male students in the program, the administration bent over backward to keep male students in the program—that was the privilege part. But the other side of it was that there were really no expectations for him. Because he was a Person of Color, the stereotype was that he had more stresses in his life and, therefore, they would make more accommodations without realizing that would be fine if they still had a certain standard for assessing his competency.

I asked Frances how she thinks people who are more accommodating to students of color can transcend the types of stereotypical assumptions that resulted in low expectations for the student she described.

The transcending comes from their own critical conscience. The whole way in which culture is taught in schools, it's taught in a very superficial, neutral way. Social work educators don't have to consider their own level of consciousness or standpoint. It's just skin deep. Unless critical race theory becomes part of what the students have to learn, people teaching the courses won't have to be at a different level. You can't teach critical race theory, you can't teach multiculturalism from a critical race perspective, unless you have a conscience that's at that level. The social work profession is at a fault line unless it is able to grapple with the ideas of power and privilege, both in the methodology of teaching and in the content of what students are taught.

Frances described practices that challenge the types of White privilege that permeate conventional social service interventions:

> Segregation is so insidious that even the way we define problems is a segregated forum. The way in which we look at bringing groups together, for example, is segregated. We bring groups together defined by their presenting problem, whether it's children with attention deficit disorder or divorced mothers or single mothers. That whole mental health system of categorization is isomorphic to the segregation and the domination that this culture is immersed in.
>
> When we think about community at our agency, we think about a diverse community that has to come together so that barriers of segregation are broken down, because I don't think you can transcend White privilege as long as we live in segregated communities. We are doing a position paper that we're really struggling with, because one of the things we're saying is basically that social justice, the social justice paradigm, is absolutely a necessity in the 21st century and that systems of accountability and empowerment have to be viewed as developmental processes in family life—just like leaving home and marriage and all the other developmental processes.
>
> We're considering having the audience consider two processes, accountability and empowerment, as central to family life. We are trying to examine how you would interview a White family, what would White therapists say to White families? Some of the questions we think they need to begin to consider are, "What communities do you live in? Whom do you live next to? Who are your friends? If you make eighty-thousand dollars, how do you think that impacts the working-class neighborhood next to you? What do you think they earn, and how are you connected?" The questions for a White isolated family have to be the other side of the knowledge. Otherwise I think we're doing very segregated

therapy. We no longer can say that we just have to do this work in order to work with the oppressed. We've got to work with the oppressors because otherwise nothing really changes. It's a first-order change.

Doc shared a story about one of his student's experiences in field education that reinforced Frances's notion that White privilege must be challenged at its source:

Let me tell you another story. I've had a student in a field placement at a municipal hospital, and the student began the placement in terrible personal condition, not physically, but socially. It was a big mess. But she was focused, she showed up, she was taking care of business, and then things fell apart again. She was about to get evicted is the bottom line, although the reasons for it are complicated.

As she was dealing with all this, which required that she deal with all sorts of city bureaucracies, including the rules about public assistance—she's got a couple of kids, she was very focused on getting this stuff done and also continuing her education. If she had to miss a day in the field placement she would e-mail me, she would call her field instructor, immediately when she came back to work she would set up a day when she could make up the time she lost, even though that redoubled the pressure on her later. All this went on, and she pretty much pulled it all together, and then as things happened with the city bureaucracy it all collapsed again, and so she faced the potential of being evicted all over again, and she's got the two kids, and she's running back and forth, and all this is happening.

I went to her field placement a couple of times, and the last time I went out to the hospital in mid-February or so, I and the field instructor and the student sat down and caught our breath and determined things looked like they're in good shape. We worked out a plan for making up whatever hours she had missed. Her field instructor and I congratulated her for always being responsible about notifying and being committed to the process.

Then a week ago she gets this disparaging evaluation, which basically said, "You had all these problems." I called up the field instructor and said, "Listen, I know she had all those problems. The issue is not did she have problems? The issue is did she keep up with those problems? That's the issue. Did she deal with her personal issues in a responsible and emerging professional way?" The response from the field instructor was along the lines of, "We gave her a lot of breaks all semester. We really had to bend over backwards for her."

I'm sitting there on the phone, and I had heard this the night before when the student was telling me, because the student is considering going on to graduate school, and the field instructor says, "Well maybe it's not a good idea for you, so I'm not going to write a reference letter." Well, the field instructor graduated from this program, by the way, and while she was in college she dealt with her health issues and her kids' health issues, and she got through it all.

The field instructor is White and the student is not. I kept thinking, "What is this? I've given you enough of a break. Who are you to say I've given you enough of a break?" I didn't say that. What I did say was, "We sat down, and we talked this thing through, and if you had an objection to how the student dealt with stuff, the time to raise that objection was with me when we were working out a plan of action. But you never did that. As a matter of fact, you said that you commended her for always notifying people and being flexible enough to make up her hours. So what is this pulling the rug out from under the person at the last minute?" Anyway, the field instructor wrote the letter of recommendation for the student to get into graduate school. But frankly, she wrote the letter because I was her teacher years ago in one class, and I said, "You don't know what you're talking about. Just write the letter because if you don't write the letter it's devastating. Even if you write a lukewarm letter that's fine. We can finesse that."

What a terrible thing to pull the rug out from under the person at the end from the point of view, "I've had enough giving you breaks." It's not a question of breaks. That's the issue of privilege right there, where suddenly you find out it's not a matter of contracting, it's not a matter of discussing, it's not a matter of mutually planning. There is no mutuality. There is, "I am keeping secret tabs on how long a leash I'm going to give you." I use that word *leash* advisedly. "How long the leash is going to be. Then at the last minute, literally at the last minute, this was last Monday, I decide to yank it back because I gave you long enough and what? You didn't achieve a total turnaround in your personal life?" The issue is the student put in all the hours, and by the way, she's a wonderful interviewer.

REGENERATION: RESOURCES, TOOLS, AND STRATEGIES FOR PROLONGED ENGAGEMENT

Regeneration refers to the activities, beliefs, and sources of support that sustain prolonged engagement in counterhegemonic social work education and practice. The challenges people face in regenerating critical consciousness vary depending on standpoint. Grace, for example, described how White privilege results in a luxury of choice with regard to a person's commitment to racial justice:

I remember once going and sitting out on the steps and saying, I'm too old for this. I don't want to do this anymore. That's part of the process, too, you get discouraged sometimes. When I get discouraged, I immediately think about the students who communicate feeling discouraged. They're White students, and I say, "Now you can take your White privilege right now and stop working on this, because you don't have to do it." What keeps me working on it is again just saying, "I'm not going to take my privilege and go live on a mountaintop and forget all about this stuff." That's the ultimate in taking your White privilege. People of Color don't have that luxury to say, "I'm tired of it, I'm not going to do this anymore," because they don't have a choice. Every day, they're faced with situations that confront them with the inequities, even if they're subtle. I can avoid this topic all together if I want to.

Kathryn described the importance of collegial networks:

> I think that no matter what kind of work I do, I find I have to have other people whom I know are supportive and who are leading me and who are guiding me and teaching me all the time. I think it's absolutely key, particularly for people who are in privileged positions, to find other allies who are in this privileged position who are continuing to move on. Because otherwise it would be like, "Oh well, I give up." For people in privileged positions it would be easier to come to that decision, to give up. I find I do have to have at least one other person with me, beside me, ahead of me, guiding me, supporting me.

The preceding excerpts focused on how White privilege includes an element of seduction to acquiesce to a racist status quo. Mateo noted how social work students can be affected by the seduction of White privilege:

> Students were saying, "Well, people aren't going to change. You're not going to change deeply ingrained racist attitudes." So I said, "Well, then we're all frauds. What are we doing here? If you don't believe that people can change, then why are we here?" The class I am thinking about responded by saying they realized how much bull they were handing out at that moment. I challenged the class. I said, "If you really don't think people are going to change, what makes you think that you're going to have an impact on somebody who was molested as a child, significantly over a period of time. Just what do you think you're going to do for that person? Are you *ever* going to change that he or she had that experience of being molested as a kid? No, you're not going change it." I pushed

them. I said, "So what are you doing? So what do you think you can do for that person? How is that different from dealing with issues of racism and oppression?" The students started to squirm uncomfortably when they realized that they were taking the easy way out by saying, "Well, you know, people don't change."

The other thing I help students think about is that it took hundreds of years to create racism. We're not going to dismantle it with one profound intervention. Do you know what I mean? Students want the one thing that's going to address racism. Such as, if you're my therapist and you're someone White, and I'm Latino or Black, let's deal with the one issue about race and then put that aside. I tell them, "Come on, it took several hundred years to get this going, so what makes you think one intervention in an interviewing session is going to dismantle it? It's a process."

Frances underscored the significance of supportive professional networks:

There does come a point in social work education when there needs to be a strong coalition between White educators and educators of color, outside of getting permission from the dean to do certain things. That kind of activism, even within academia, is really important to keep the ideas alive.

It's very hard, as I told you before, for other academicians to really value this work because, as one of my colleagues said, "If they begin to think critically they have to rethink their entire paradigm." So it's difficult unless people have worked with you or have these values. They don't necessarily want to attempt to shift the way they're working. The people who are controlling the social work knowledge base, they're the gatekeepers. They monitor what goes into and [stays] out of the journals, and so a lot of younger people who would probably be very interested in working this way don't have access to information to even consider it.

The faculty at the institution where I was employed were not able to see what I had to offer the social work community. I shouldn't say the whole faculty, because there were a couple of faculty who were terrific. But those faculty have also not been respected by the dean in that system. The fact that they were not, as a leading school of social work, able to see what I had to offer is tragic. I don't think it's about me personally. I think that's what happens in academia, which leads back to the question you asked earlier: "What can we do to recruit talented academics of color?" Well, if this is the process that's occurring, social work education is not going to have people like me in academic positions because they actively work to get rid of us.

Like Frances, Kathryn's career choices were shaped by resistance to her standpoint:

It may be necessary to change institutions, especially if you're an assistant professor, because you have to recognize who you are and what your power base is, and as assistant professors we have to recognize that the institution does have more power than we do. So it may be necessary to leave if there is absolutely no support in the institution. I have done that when I felt that I was the only one operating from a critical perspective.

I did not feel that I could actually really be who I was until I had already accepted a new position, and then in my last semester, there I was more who I was. Just speaking from my own position as an assistant professor, you have to be aware of the reality of the limitations and the constraints based on that group membership of being an assistant professor and not having tenure and being granted or not granted tenure by those who have different political views. Now I feel that I can be more open about my political perspective because I do have support from people who have tenure, and that's reality.

Mateo revealed how institutional support can promote regeneration:

> I used to coordinate the racism and oppression course. One of the things I noticed about these courses and the things I was reading is that traditionally in schools of social work, racism and oppression courses are taught by minority, adjunct faculty. The faculty's status, for example, being adjunct, means a lot, because it's a way of communicating the legitimacy of the course and the curricula. The reason that someone's race matters is because, as one person said to me, "I don't have particular expertise in this area. Because I've lived it doesn't mean I have an expertise. My expertise is child welfare." So expecting faculty of color to teach this course can become a way of ghettoizing faculty.
>
> One of the things that I insisted on when I chaired the sequence was that the faculty would represent everybody, so that it wasn't just Black people teaching the course on racism. It was White, Black, and Brown, male and female, gay and straight. Every level of professorship taught that course. The dean taught it for two years. I defy you to find another social work program, where the dean, who is a straight, White, male, teaches the racism and oppression course.
>
> When I used to have new faculty teach that course, I would always say, "Now, really understand that no matter what category you represent, you're going to be challenged on your legitimacy to teach this content." So if you're of color, usually what happens is people say, "Well, you're just angry, and you're grinding your ax." So you get dismissed out of hand that way. If you're White, it's like, "Well, what do you know?" When the dean taught this course, who like I said is a White male, his response was perfect. He would say, "Racism is not a Black person's problem, it's a White person's problem. We all have pieces in this, and we have to acknowledge and take responsibility for some parts of it."

What we did in our program was give the racism and oppression course the same status as the other course sequences. Most programs have the traditional sequences like practice, policy, research, theory. The racism and oppression course, if you look at the curriculum at most schools, they sometimes fit it in the practice sequence, sometimes the courses are in the human behavior sequence. Our course stands alone like a sequence of its own. So the coordinator of the racism and oppression sequence, like the chairs of the practice, human behavior in the social environment, and research sequences, they're always at all the meetings with equal status.

Grace also discussed the role of institutional support in regeneration:

You need the support of knowing that other people are thinking about some of the same issues. One of the best ways to do that is [to] purposefully schedule all sections of the class at the same time on the same day. At our institution we schedule all four classes at the same time on the same day. That way we can do things together in the auditorium with all of our classes. We can plan the syllabus together, and at 11:30 when class lets out, we come to my office and we have box lunches waiting, and we spend an hour and a half processing our experiences. That level of support is tremendous. Our time together may sometimes be a gripe session about a student who acted out or whom you're struggling with. We also talk about, since we're a diverse group, how students react to us differently based on our power position, both because of skin color and ethnicity and position in the school.

I think that if you taught any course, if you taught human behavior in the social environment or policy, that if you have a school big enough where there's more than one section, that it's helpful to make a conscious effort to find ways together to incorporate this material into the courses. The best way to learn about this content yourself is to teach it. If you teach content related to power and privilege, issues come up. If you have peer support, you can do critical debriefing with your colleagues after the subject has come up in the classroom and talk about how you handled it and debrief about what could you have done differently, what would you do differently next time, what did you learn from it? I think it's hard to do that alone.

Doc added that personal relationships are also an important source of regeneration:

I have a very close friend, and for years we have had lunch together every Friday afternoon. This friend, Rick, was my first supervisor going back 30 years ago. Rick is African American. I can't tell you how many times over the course of the 30 years we've been in a particular social setting where he will gesticulate or motion or make some sort of gesture or say something to a waiter, which essentially says can I have your attention, and the guy will walk past him. I will do a less significant gesture, a less grandiose gesture, "Yes sir, can I help you?" I can't tell you how many times I've seen this. I can't imagine being ignored like that and having to put up with that trivial, but nevertheless constant, trampling of who you are.

Part of Alicia's regeneration was grounded in the diversity that has been a strong feature in her life:

I would not have done a PhD were it not for a close friend, who began her PhD after her MSW. Being close to her, having a friendship with her, opened my eyes a lot to the struggles and conflicts around diversity issues. So yes, friendships are important. I remember clearly in the 1960s when I was going through social work school about being aware that one measure of my values on diversity would be looking at who my friends are and who is in my home. Who I spend time with and how diverse those friendships are. I can say over the years there has been much diversity in my life.

Mateo also connected the cultural pluralism in his personal life to the regeneration of conscientization:

> One of our leaders around here did a presentation for the students, and he said to the students, "I want you to think about who would come to your funeral. Who would be there? Who would you see?" He was talking about if you've only got one group of people coming to your funeral, you really haven't lived a multicultural life. I've been intrigued by that notion of who would be at my funeral, and it would be a wide range of people. Different colors, different ethnic backgrounds, different economic backgrounds, different religions, different sexual orientations. It would be interesting, and that represents what I have tried to construct in my life.

CONSCIENTIZATION: PERCEPTIONS AND BEHAVIOR GROUNDED IN CRITICAL ANALYSES

Conscientization results from perpetual interactions among development, application, and regeneration. Conscientization denotes understanding how privilege and oppression correspond and challenging both. Mateo described how he talks with his students about neutralizing and transcending privilege:

> Maybe it's been the circumstances in my life that there's been somebody when I needed it who stepped up to the plate and protected me or called somebody on the carpet for doing something to me around a certain thing. It's my belief that I need to pass that on. I say to students, "You're going to recognize that you have some privilege, and this isn't about guilt. You can sit there and beat your chest and say how terrible you feel, but then that's another excuse not to act, because you get so immobilized. Okay, you've got some benefits in your life, good for you. Now how are

you going to use them?" I say, "Kick the door open for somebody. Because you're going to be in places where you got there because of your privilege, and you're going to look around and certain people aren't there. It's your voice that counts for something." I turn to White students and say, "For you as a White person to challenge racism, even when there's nobody Black or Latino there, says something." I turn to the men and say, "For you men to ac-knowledge that you have privilege by being male and to challenge sexism says something. It changes it." I emphasize to students, "You can do those things from your position of power, and what you are trying to do is share power."

The interaction between awareness of one's privileged statuses and conscious-ness and behaviors was a topic that Grace addressed as well:

Understanding the White side of the equation totally changed the way I approached oppression. Instead of it becoming a cause to help people who've been impacted by racism, it became "We're all in this together and it isn't their problem, it's our problem." I'd always given lip service before to "it's a White problem," but for some reason, to understand psychologically what happens to White people didn't happen until I discovered Peggy McIntosh's work. I remember her paper on White privilege and male privi-lege, even when it was in draft form, and it totally changed my perspective.

It's like there are things that I can do that I never thought about because I didn't know how much I had benefited myself. It has also helped me to understand peoples' blind spots and the dynamics in the classroom between students of color and White students. The students of color may have to sit and listen to people discover things that are so obvious to them. We talk about that very directly in my classes. That's where the whole concept of White privilege has really been helpful, is in exposing that whole thing of not needing to know about privilege is a privilege. It also exposes the oppression in why People of Color have to know about privilege for survival, being the people who don't have the privilege, the position that they've been in.

Another privilege is you get to choose whether or not you're going to say, "I've had enough of this talk about oppression and injustice, and I don't want to hear anymore." That is a White privilege. You can say, "Well, I've learned about racism, and now I'm not going to pay any attention to it." People of Color don't have that privilege. Every minute of every day they are faced with having to be made aware of their social identity and what that means.

Students feel terribly, terribly guilty because they say, "But I didn't know, and I feel so bad that I'm White." I say, "One of your privileges was not knowing. It was kept from you, too. That's one of the ways it works is it's kept from you. It's not in the newspaper."

Alicia described how the process of conscientization exposes myths that protect and perpetuate White privilege:

Regarding White racism, one of the barriers to understanding White racism is the idea of People of Color being racist. There's still a lot of confusion [about] or an unwillingness to look at what the nature of racism is in the United States. Specifically that it is institutional in nature. When we talk about racism, we're talking about patterns in society, such as access to housing, education, and health care. This perspective asserts that individuals can be racist and not be prejudiced. Racism is about business as usual. Racism is about carrying out practices that are institutionalized that have very clear consequences, racist consequences, particularly in terms of segregation, but do not require prejudiced people to carry those policies out.

There isn't enough discussion about racism and the confusion about what racism is. Perhaps the emphasis on individualism in this country results in racism being looked at as an individual, psychological phenomenon. By that I mean that the power differences between individuals get overlooked. Latinos are viewed as racist, rather than prejudiced and discriminatory, when they aggress on other ethnic groups. What gets lost is the context in terms of domination and social power. Part of the problem is a tendency to look at racism from a psychological, individual point of view. Also, because Euro-Americans are, by and large, in a position of power, White racism is a major issue to address.

It's not to say all Euro-Americans are racist. Well, let me backtrack a bit. An assumption I make in all of my classes is that all of us have been exposed to racism and have internalized it. That isn't the issue. When it comes to working on racism, the issue is what is someone doing about learning about how we have been individually affected by racism? I mean everyone, including People of Color, have internalized racism from different points of view.

McIntosh's insightful writing focused specifically on the entitlements that accompany White privilege. She described things like knowing when you walk into a reception area, if you have privilege or entitlement, you have a very different experience in terms of recognition and responsiveness. It's still a very sensitive issue, and we probably haven't found good ways to talk about that yet.

Frances introduced additional concepts related to structural inequalities:

Our training program involves learning both about the self in context and clients in context. That requires students to engage in work to understand their standpoint through their own gender, race, class, sexual orientation, and culture. Because this is not about dissecting the clients in the room. It's about looking at parallel systems and the isomorphism between privilege and oppression and how structural inequalities affect peoples' lives. We've had people who've been completely thrilled and excited about our training program, and it's been both White and non-White students.

Conscientization is an ongoing process of learning and acting with the intention of applying enduring resistance to structural inequalities. Incorporating critical discourse in social work education can evoke an educator's conscientization. It can also reinforce or catalyze the conscientization of students.

ACADEMIC SYNERGY: ARTICULATING CONSCIENTIZATION IN SOCIAL WORK EDUCATION

Academic synergy results from engaged pedagogy. Mateo revealed a type of reflexive engagement that promoted academic synergy:

> Do students think that they're going to be graded on their racism or their sexism? That isn't what the grade is about. Because you know what? We're all racist. We're all sexist. We're all . . . whatever, now that we've been through that, let's understand what that means. As social workers, we're supposed to be able to meet the needs of a changing world, and that means that we in the academy have to rethink our positions. It's not to say the positions and views we outgrew were all bad, or they're useless, but some of them were of another time and lacked reflection. For me, one of the big things about education is that I will not ask a student to do something that I am unwilling to do. So if I'm asking students to engage in a process of self-reflection, then I have to join them in that, and so it's sort of a Freire model of collaborative education and cooperative education.
>
> The full-time faculty where I work get it. We struggle with our own painful conversations, and I think the important piece is this has to be sort of a community-wide commitment to these conversations, creating fear-free zones. What I mean by that is,

"Okay, let people ask the questions that may feel offensive to others." They can't get the answers if you're busy slamming them down. This is what I love about the institution where I teach. It's not been easy, there have been tears, there's been yelling in faculty meetings, there's been hair pulling and throat clutching. But we all have a shared vision of what we want this place to look like, and we struggle with it, because it's not easy.

I have to give it to this faculty. They time and again come right back to it. We drift away from it, because things get tense or we focus on other interests, but we come right back to it. We collectively ask ourselves, "Are we doing what we say we're doing? What is it that we're trying to do? Who do we say that we are, and how do we live this out, not just in terms of teaching our students, but how do we live it in community?"

Rita discussed a strategy for engaging students in critical thinking about professional scholarship:

I teach a course in the doctoral program on writing for publication, and I built social justice into that course by saying, "If we believe that the core purpose of social work is social justice, then we need to think about, does this piece of research, does this piece of writing, advance social justice?" With the idea being that's a way of choosing one's focus, of choosing priorities, and so forth.

Grace described how she used the pro-con articles from the *Journal of Social Work Education* to promote academic synergy:

I taught a PhD course about preparing for academia that focused on issues in social work and social work education. In that course we examined issues where there are pros and cons within the profession and within social work education and dealt with it that way. The *Journal of Social Work Education* has those pro–con articles, so we drew on those as much as we could.

We looked at areas like cultural diversity. Affirmative action in higher education is another area. Should it be women's studies or gender studies is another one. Should religion, diversity of religion, be incorporated into social work curriculum, the pros and cons of that. I infused critical analysis by having students consider issues that are under conflict within the profession. Multiculturalism in social work, what does that look like? The students really got into looking at what are the differences of opinion within the profession on these things. We even considered if there is a discrete social work set of values to which everybody in the profession adheres. The students always thought the answer to that was yes and that everybody agreed, at least on the core values. When we started to break that down, I think they were pretty fascinated and saw rich areas for research and writing.

Frances talked about the importance of providing students with catalysts that move them beyond awareness:

It has been my experience repeatedly that people with White privilege do not move beyond awareness. Recognizing that they, too, have been manipulated is one part of the work, but it doesn't stop there. There needs to be talk, because that is part of the process for identifying what's going on—that's the truth telling. But then there needs to be some kind of reparation before you go to what's forgiveness or resolution.

I find that people of privilege want to move from truth to resolution, sort of jumping over this whole section that challenges them to consider reparations, in order to be in the fray with People of Color in the coalition. That's the piece that I think the whole White privilege discourse has not moved to, really articulating what it means to have or speak about economic reparations. What does it really mean to share power and not continue to have a cognitive conversation about reparation but still hold power over others? That whole idea of how to remember is very important regardless of whether your hands actually held the blood of another. Very much like the Germans and the Jews after the Holocaust, remembering is about justice. Remembering and then sort of paying some sort of retribution is a way of creating a new collective conscience.

In the work I am doing with some of my colleagues, we're saying basically that social justice, the social justice paradigm, of course, is absolutely a necessity in the 21st century and that systems of accountability and empowerment have to be viewed as developmental processes in family life. We essentially want to talk reparations and what it means to begin to have that conversation. So talking about reparations for African Americans, but then how do we raise that issue with the White families in therapy in order to raise their consciousness? We're looking at many different things, because the whole idea, you're probably familiar with what happened in South Africa—that project failed miserably because it was based on truth and resolution, and they talked about reparative justice, but they never actually introduced reparations.

They talked about the idea that all Whites would be taxed for a considerable number of years and the taxation would all go to families of color, towards the schools, their neighborhoods, that sort of thing. They talked about some ways each community would be redistricted so that the land would be returned to the Indigenous Peoples. Well, a lot of that hasn't happened. People would go down and pour their hearts out about what they did, and several of the police actually confessed to all the brutal crimes they committed, but there was no reparation, and the whole system fell apart because the remembering itself wasn't substantive enough. There was no economic shift that went with it.

There's a great writer who has written a fabulous book on the whole notion of reparations. He essentially says we can talk about reparations but we first have to talk about the communities within Africa, for example, really beginning to take responsibility for the thugs who have controlled the politics in many African countries and killed their own people, and that within-group healing has to occur while we're demanding some kind of reparation in the form of economic repayment or an economic sort of redistricting. That the global exporting system moves in one direction for a while—those kinds of things.

In the United States what a lot of African Americans are talking about is, just for example, in every community having several Black institutions that would be Black run, Black owned, and the money would go directly into the Black community. The other idea, which you may have heard, is the notion of having a whole federal education system so that the school districts would not be tax-bound, and they would all be nationalized and with the level of education and the computer systems across communities, all of that would be exactly the same.

Alicia provided a strategy for talking to students about engagement:

It may not be that we do it, but we may want to support others who do, or we may want to encourage our professional organizations to get involved. I mean that's the first thing, being aware of the historical moment. I guess the other piece of that is being aware of what's going on regionally, statewide, as well, in terms of bigger issues.

Students need to know that refusing to participate in White solidarity is a reparative act of resistance.

Sleeter (1996) used the term "White racial bonding" to refer to "interactions that have the purpose of affirming a common stance on race-related issues, legitimating particular interpretations of oppressed groups, and drawing we-they boundaries" (p. 261). Kathryn described how she resisted White racial bonding:

I know one of the things that came up recently was that I was in a meeting and someone made a comment about, "What do you do to help so many students of color who can't write well?" I used that opportunity to say, "It's been my experience that a lot of White students can't write well either. So I think it's a different issue, and we need to reframe the issue to look at what can we do to help all students learn to write well."

SUMMARY

Discourse regarding White privilege exposes the structural nature of racism in the United States. It is the type of discourse that emanates from and can be a catalyst for transformational critical consciousness. Social work educators who have not explored the contemporary discourse regarding White privilege can begin by considering the standpoint from which U.S. history has been created. According to Zinn (1999), the choices historians make about which facts to emphasize in telling U.S. history are ideological in nature. The "historian has been trained in a society in which education and knowledge are put forward as technical problems of excellence and not as tools for contending social classes, races, and nations" (Zinn, p. 8). Alternatively, Zinn provided a critical perspective about U.S. history through *A People's History of the United States: 1492–Present.*

White privilege and racism are not impermeable features of the national landscape in the United States. They are, however, a legacy that we have inherited, and they are prominent aspects of our daily lives. Perkinson (2002) suggested, "education is a process of evolution or growth—intellectual and social growth" (p. 365). Recognizing the fallibility of our knowledge provides the opportunity to grow beyond our limitations. Perkinson reminded us that "criticism facilitates this growth" (p. 365). The social work profession is committed to effecting "social and economic justice worldwide" (Council on Social Work Education [CSWE], 2001, p. 2). Discourse regarding White privilege is a significant resource for promoting deeper analyses of the mechanisms that perpetuate structural inequalities.

CHAPTER 3

Reflexivity and Transparency

As I contemplated the participants' responses to my interview questions, I realized they shared commonalities in terms of being reflexive and transparent. Following this realization, I grouped excerpts from each person's transcripts that characterized reflexivity and transparency and analyzed those chunks of data. Reflexivity involves deliberate analyses of experiences with the goal of reaching consciousness that potentiates deeper understandings and choices about future thoughts and behaviors (Danielewicz, 2001; Finlay & Gough, 2003). Transparency is a mechanism instructors can use to preserve clarity about their expectations. Rita's reflexivity surfaced through the following observation:

> I think everybody has grown and matured and understands things differently. At this point, faculty whom I teach with are more sophisticated about things like racial identity development for both Whites and People of Color. I have a strong sense of this being a developmental process for everybody—a lifelong developmental process.

Grace exemplified reflexivity when she described evolution in her approach to teaching:

> I used to get very frustrated with students. I was quite self-righteous when I first started teaching full time in 1980. I was involved in causes, and I thought that I had the truth with a capital *T*. The truth! I found that students were either already with me, because my truth was their truth, too, which was great. Or they fought me because it wasn't their truth, and they weren't

going to buy it. Sometimes they just shut down and didn't say anything.

At one point in the early 1980s, I went through some faculty development workshops, and the man who was the head of the faculty development office commented to me, "Grace, you have your own process, and what you need to tell the students is that it's yours and they can't have it."

This man was very clever, because he let me know that if my students had my process, they were stealing it from me. But what that helped me see was that if I imposed my process on students, I was stealing from them. He helped me see that students had their own life journey and their own process, and they were going to have many people along the way who were going to play a role in that process, and I was only one of them. That was one thing that was helpful to me.

The other thing is that my truth keeps changing. If I look back at what I believed, even five years ago, I can shake my head and wonder, "How could I have thought that? I know something different now." So, if I'm in a developmental process, and I keep changing, then I have to trust that students are as well.

In fact, differences in students' development came out last Friday in class when we were talking about women's issues. We were talking about women's issues across races and ages and all other identity characteristics. One student told a story about when she was in business. She's an older student and she got promoted to an executive level. She was the first woman to have gotten promoted to that level, and one of the first things one of her male colleagues said to her was, "Well, now that you've gotten this position, the first thing you need to do is go through initiation. That means you need to get naked in the hot tub with all of us." She didn't know what to say. This was many years ago, and even in class all these years later she was embarrassed to talk about it. She blushed in class.

One of the male students said, "Why didn't you tell him that was offensive to you?" I swear, every woman in the class took a different stab at trying to explain how complicated it was and how they understood why she didn't speak up right then, and this well-meaning man just couldn't get it. How do we talk about that? In that class we talked about the privilege of not getting it. I said to him, "All these women who talked, they need to understand what it's about and they need to get it, but you don't have to. You're faced with a decision about whether you're going to open yourself up and try to hear the voices of the oppressed, even though it doesn't coincide with your experience, and consider the possibility that it's real. You can choose to open yourself up to that or not. You have the privilege of making a decision about whether or not you will listen to your classmates."

I challenged him not to invoke his privilege by dismissing what his classmates were trying to tell him. To invoke your privilege not to pay attention to the voice of the oppressed is colluding with injustice.

Alicia characterized reflexivity when she talked about influences that can affect students' responses to discourse regarding White privilege:

The idea is for students to recognize the presence of social power and how it functions and how it affects peoples' lives. This gets people looking at their own history and their own awareness, or lack of awareness, about social power and awareness of privilege, oftentimes for the first time—certainly for Euro-American students. Students often have fears that they will be judged or criticized by others, but I think mainly by themselves, because these are students with good intentions going into social work. Faculty need to be aware that students experience a sense of loss, a loss of the old self, a loss of who they thought they were in this transition to a more developed person who's now incorporating these other aspects of him- or herself, like their social identity, into their self-concept.

It's important to get a class to the point where they are willing to take risks by talking about very private, personal issues—conflicts they have about diversity, for instance. In racism classes I taught, students would often talk about growing up in all-White neighborhoods and not having any contact with People of Color until they were in higher education. Students often have to deal with their family's beliefs and values. At some point, many students deal with conflicts that come up for them as they take a critical look at their parents and grandparents.

Faculty who teach from a critical perspective have to value knowing themselves, knowing their own history, and they have to appreciate the type of teaching that conveys openness—personal and professional openness. Professors need to see teaching as an interactive process that involves their being intellectually and emotionally present and open with the students. Faculty must be willing to struggle with all of the intensity in the classroom. I expect a benefit of teaching from a critical perspective is the amount of change that an educator can see within the classroom and in individual students.

Doc personified reflexivity when he discussed the complexity of students' lives:

Something occurred to me in my work with clients after I got my master's degree. I was working in an intensive service program. I was expected to see every client's family three or four times a month. It occurred to me that if I saw each family two hours a week—which is a lot—that left 166 hours for other influences to play out in their lives. Two hours on one hand, 166 hours on the other. I am suddenly very humbled by how little I know and how little I can do. To me, that was always a strong argument for understanding social work as working with the client, because you can't do anything to somebody in two hours a week that could possibly countervail the other 166 hours of influence.

I start off thinking that my impact on people is limited—and not limited in a self-depreciatory way. People have their own lives. I take that perspective into my work with students as well, because there's a lot about their lives that I don't know. There's a lot about what they're struggling with that I don't know, and that's even true of students who are open and looking for guidance and support.

Mateo's reflexivity emerged through an account of classroom dynamics:

When people walk into a racism and oppression class, they're immediately dividing people up into good people, bad people. You're the racist. I'm not. Having seen this, I say at the beginning of a new class, "There will be no witch hunt for the racist in this room." Because what happens, particularly with groups of White students, is they look for the one person to raise the naive question or to put out things that are really in fact racist, and then they pounce on that person.

If you get the notion of what an *ism* is, we're all guilty. There are no innocent bystanders. We all have a piece in it. I challenge students to do a lot of self-examination. I say to the students, "You want to work with people, and you're going to have hard conversations with clients, and you can't have them with your colleagues without being defensive or judgmental? What's that about? That's another piece of feeling like you have more power than the other person. The conversations we have in this classroom can teach you things you need to know when you are working with clients and things you need to do out there in the world, in terms of changing the world."

I establish ground rules at the beginning of the semester. You have the right to have all kinds of feelings. You don't have the right to call anybody a name. You don't have any right to threaten anyone. When people start having intense conversations I will say, "I'm here to help facilitate the conversation." So when it starts to get too heated and people aren't listening to each other, I might say, "Okay, I want everyone to stop at this moment and take a deep breath."

What usually happens when people become upset or angry is that the conversation changes. They may not say, "I'm angry at you because what you said hurt my feelings." Instead it's like, "What kind of a person would say *X* about whatever?" It's removed in some way. So I will stop people and say, "Ask a question. Don't make a statement. What's the question that you want to ask this person?"

Kathryn described how she required her students to practice reflexivity and transparency through course assignments:

I have assignments that require students to look at their feelings, to look at their intellectual learning, and to analyze and articulate their actions. That kind of self-reflection is a requirement I always work into assignments. I include self-reflection in every assignment, and I evaluate the effectiveness of my instruction on the basis of how well students communicate self-reflection.

This excerpt suggested to me that reflexivity and transparency were features of the participants' pedagogy that promoted academic synergy. Frances's data provided support for this conceptual leap:

At our agency, we use the same strategies with our clients and our students to begin to shift what I call a false consciousness. We use films and specific readings to deconstruct the way our social order currently exists. We use information that demonstrates how the current social order is a social, political order and that the way we think about gender, race, class, and sexual orientation are all ways in which society organizes us in relationship to one another. So that's the first step where we get students thinking about false consciousness in the process of developing critical consciousness.

We might show something like *Pretty Woman* and *Jungle Fever* juxtaposed with one another. Then we talk about the whole idea of *Pretty Woman* and how Julia Roberts, in spite of being a sex industry worker, gets to be in a position of privilege with Richard Gere, unlike her African American counterpart in *Jungle Fever,* who never leaves the streets. We question students about what that means and why the status of the women in those movies is different. Usually at the beginning both clients and students will say, "Well, it's different because Julia Roberts is beautiful, it's because, because, because . . .," without really looking at the deeper construct of that whole story.

Then we might use another film, for example, show a fairy tale like *The Little Mermaid*. In *The Little Mermaid*, Ariel, who's a very slender, White-skinned, anorexic-looking young mermaid, makes a deal with Ursula the witch, who's this looming, big, heavyset woman who's supposed to be the strength that allows Ariel the power to marry the prince. Ariel is making a deal with Ursula, and so in that whole depiction, which is about five and a half minutes, you begin to see all of the social location issues that we've been talking about.

When students start to develop consciousness, they get to a point of being able to see, for example, the way in which the idea of beauty is set up—to see which traditional notion of marriage is universalized, to see how strength in women is depicted as evil, dark-skinned, and ugly, which is very much reflective of how women of color are reflected. All of those subtleties and not so subtle things are what students and clients can pick up after they get the consciousness of what it means to be socially located.

Doc discussed how transparency countervails privilege:

> I love that transparency has become a big word in the last half-dozen years, because I think it's an effective and understandable political idea and a good way of measuring things in terms of the goal of social justice, because it's the lack of transparency that reinforces privilege and arbitrary authority.
>
> When I was working on my MSW, a teacher asked, "Why shouldn't your clients be able to read their own case records?" This was a question that parted the Red Sea for me, because I couldn't think of a single reason why not. The whole class was outraged at the idea that a client should be able to read his or her own records, but I sat there thinking, Well, why not? Because presumably everything that's in the records happened or is something that the client said or is something that you said. So why shouldn't the client be able to read the account? I sat there thinking, what an incredible idea.
>
> I throw that out sometimes in trainings and usually once a year or so in school, and people are outraged by the idea. Since social workers would likely write their records differently if they viewed clients as part of the audience, that tells you how privilege is being exercised in the writing of the records.

A parallel to the type of transparency Doc discussed is for an educator to make as clear as possible to students the standpoint he or she is teaching from, which was something Mateo talked about:

> I tell my students, "I have theoretical and professional preferences. I'm not asking you to have the same preferences. I'm telling you about my professional standpoint. You can decide for yourself where you stand."

Alicia suggested that self-disclosure can be an effective strategy for promoting transparency:

I think faculty modeling, by sharing as much of my experience as I can, is important. It communicates opening the door and to some extent normalizing some things that may be difficult for students to talk about. But I think educators have to do a lot of work on themselves to be able to share their experiences and think on their feet in order to respond to the issues that students are struggling with.

As Grace revealed, however, self-disclosures can have unintended consequences:

In terms of self-disclosure, I'm still playing around with it in terms of how much to self-disclose. The first day of class I usually ask everybody to write down on a piece of paper, "I am . . . and then whatever words come." Then I ask them to share as much information as they are comfortable with in the very first class session. I start out by modeling the level of self-disclosure I'm comfortable with, and I am always uncertain about how much self-disclosure is too much too soon.

I remember in one undergraduate practicum seminar there were about 12 students in the class. We did an exercise similar to that at the beginning, and we talked about race and ethnicity and how that affects our worldviews and our life experiences. I too quickly disclosed that I felt that if you were White you could not avoid participating in racism because of White privilege. A Black student went to the BSW program director and said, "I can't be in the class because the professor is racist and she admits it." The BSW director had a sense of what was going on and talked to the student about what I might be saying and suggested the three of us talk about it. The three of us did talk about it, and I realized that my self-disclosure was too big and too soon.

I still struggle with when to self-disclose with students. The guideline for me is, will it facilitate students' learning? Not, what do I need to do for me? Because I consider that to be a boundary violation if I'm doing it for me—just as with a client and a social worker,

> if the social worker's self-disclosing for the social worker's sake—I
> think that's a boundary violation. I struggle with knowing when it
> will help students with their learning and when it will inhibit it.

Once I perceived the importance of reflexivity and transparency in promoting academic synergy, I realized the model of transformational critical consciousness could be expanded by adding the principles of participant action education to articulate strategies for promoting critical thought. Social work educators who operate from a standpoint grounded in transformational critical consciousness can use the principles of participant action education to encourage and support their students' conscientization.

PRINCIPLES OF PARTICIPANT ACTION EDUCATION

The principles of participant action education are an adaptation of the key features of participant action research discussed by Kemmis and McTaggart (2000):

- The educational process is organized around individual and collective attempts to understand how identity is shaped by society.
- The educational process is participatory, and students are encouraged to examine the origins of their knowledge and the bases for their interpretations and to consider how the origins of their knowledge and the bases of their interpretations shape their worldviews.
- The educational process promotes educational collaboration between the teacher and students and collaboration among students that is independent of the teacher.
- The educational process challenges the grand narratives that are undergirded by and perpetuate White privilege and other forms of oppression and exploitation.
- The educational process promotes critical thinking that can be applied in social work practice.
- The educational process empowers students to engage in social transformation.

The principles of participant action education embody a dynamic pedagogical orientation that requires educators and students to engage in ongoing critical reflection. The relationships between transformational critical consciousness and the principles of participant action education are depicted in Figure 2.

FIGURE 2: Model of Participant Action Education

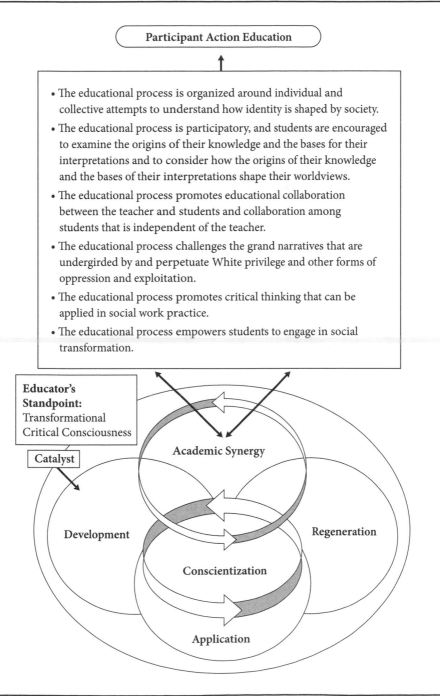

Participant action education is a critical pedagogical approach that promotes ongoing, active reflection on the part of educators and students and belies the notion that social work education is an objective, passive transfer of knowledge. Engagement between the teacher and students and collaboration among students that is independent of the teacher facilitates the ongoing generation of knowledge. The other principles of participant action education promote power analyses of structural inequalities that reveal corresponding relationships between privileges and oppression, as in the case of White privilege and racism.

Healy (2001) cautioned against undertaking participant action research without adequately theorizing the researchers' power to shape and benefit from their investigations. Chataway (as cited in Healy, 2001) suggested that rather than trying to erase differences in power that exist between researchers and their participants, social workers are better served by understanding the influences of existing power by observing its effects on the research. These cautions and considerations are also relevant to participant action education.

Social work educators have more power than their students do as a result of their sanction to determine what course content is important, establish how performance standards will be measured, and assign students' grades. Furthermore, the thought of being evaluated on the basis of their responses to critical content, such as content regarding White privilege, may heighten students' anxieties. These dynamics are intrinsic to higher education regardless of the degree to which they are explicated. The principles of participant action education provide a framework for creating a classroom climate where these issues can be explicated and dealt with transparently.

"Ethnocentrism is the natural tendency of people to view reality from their own cultural perspective and to believe that perspective is the most appropriate" (Weaver, 2005, p. 49). White privilege in the United States results from ethnocentrism coupled with power (Haney Lopez, 1996; Lipsitz, 1998). It is, therefore, not surprising that it can be challenging to incorporate content regarding White privilege in social work classes. Whereas White students may initially react with denial, become overwhelmed with guilt, and/or attempt to change the focus of the discussion, students of color may respond with resentment or deny the implications of White privilege (Derman-Sparks & Phillips, 1997). Boice (2000) noted that inexperienced educators are typically unprepared to deal with classroom incivilities, such as highly emotional outbursts or intimidating disagreements that make the whole class tense. Educators, experienced and novice, may be reticent to introduce content regarding White privilege into their classrooms if they have not developed the consciousness to correct common misunderstandings and address students' questions (Fox, 2001).

Social work education should emphasize that we all have a sphere of influence that can be used for effective actions against racism and White privilege (Tatum, 1997). Thus, the task for all people is to "identify what our own sphere of influence is (however large or small) and to consider how it might be used to interrupt the cycle of racism" (Tatum, p. 105). For Whites who are looking to be agents of social change, this work involves challenging systems of privilege and oppression and influencing other Whites to do the same (Tatum). The principles of participant action education provide a conceptual framework for establishing a classroom climate where students are invited to engage in a process of discovery. In dealing with content regarding White privilege, for example, the principles of participant action education promote engagement, which could be accomplished by asking students to consider the influences that insulate White privilege from examination.

SUMMARY

Critical dialogue develops intellectual habits that undermine the myths that perpetuate racism (Shor & Freire, 1987). Discourse regarding White privilege is critical dialogue. Participant action education illuminates the origins of the values and beliefs that have shaped the character of the United States and prepares citizens who can critically examine and challenge discrepancies between our stated beliefs and national behavior (Howard, 1999).

CHAPTER 4

Operationalizing Participant Action Education

Participant action education is organized around individual and collective attempts to understand how identity is shaped by society. A key to effectively incorporating discourse regarding White privilege into a class discussion or assignment is establishing the historical context for contemporary systemic advantages provided to Whites. Books, such as *Teaching and Learning Anti-Racism: A Developmental Approach* (Derman-Sparks & Phillips, 1997) and *When Race Breaks Out: Conversations about Race and Racism in College Classrooms* (Fox, 2001), offer guidance for introducing the concept of White privilege to students. An anthology of brief articles, *Readings for Diversity and Social Justice: An Anthology on Racism, Antisemitism, Sexism, Heterosexism, Ableism, and Classism*, contextualizes structural inequalities and societal oppression (Adams et al., 2000). These types of resources challenge grand narratives, such as meritocracy, and promote students' individual and collective attempts to understand how identity is shaped by society.

Light (2001) revealed that students value educators who are able to convey to students how to think like a professional. Many outstanding educators engage students by giving them opportunities to use their reasoning skills to tackle problems (Bain, 2004). Students respond positively to participatory processes that encourage them to examine the origins of their knowledge and the bases for their interpretations and to consider how the origins of their knowledge and the bases of their interpretations shape their worldviews. I have found that students are eager to engage in critical analyses and dialogue when asked to deconstruct articles like King's (1991) "Dysconscious Racism: Ideology, Identity, and the Miseducation of Teachers" and Vaz's (1995) "Racial Aliteracy: White Appropriation of Black Presences."

Adams (1997) noted that small groups provide spaces for listening and brainstorming. Students respond positively when asked to engage in structured conversation about a reading or film in a small group and then to share their small-group discussion with the class. This strategy increases class participation and promotes educational collaboration among the students that is independent of the instructor.

Democratic education encourages critical thinking. Chairs arranged in circles rather than rows facing the front of the room reinforce the imagery of co-learning (Adams, 1997). A climate where students feel like co-facilitators of learning is conducive to dialogue. Dialogue that requires critical thinking generates critical thinking (Adams). Educational processes that encourage students to participate in critical conversations can promote their empowerment for participating in problem-solving endeavors directed at social transformation (Bell, 1997).

Effective teachers know their subjects extremely well (Bain, 2004). Preparation for teaching and knowing how to engage students are fundamental elements of successful pedagogy (Bain, 2004; Boice, 2000; Light, 2001). The targeted readings suggested in Appendix A support transformational critical consciousness and recommend strategies conducive to participant action education.

Discourse regarding White privilege is critical content that social work educators can use to illuminate the structural elements of racism in the United States. The idea of incorporating content regarding White privilege into social work education may seem daunting, particularly to White social work educators who have not achieved what Howard (1999) referred to as "transformationist White identity" (p. 106). The conversations reported in this book revealed that it is a person's consciousness—rather than his or her racial identity—that inspires a willingness to explicate and confront White privilege.

Developing the confidence and skills to effectively incorporate content regarding White privilege into social work education is a perpetual process. Fox (2001) noted that she enjoyed teaching about race, racism, and White privilege once she had some conversation starters, unusual discussion formats, in-class writing assignments, role-plays, and simulations that promoted debate and critical thinking. My conversations with the participants revealed that preparation for teaching from a critical perspective requires personal reflection and participation in critical discourse.

Lorde (1984) maintained there are no new ideas, just new ways of giving breadth and power to the ideas we cherish. Exposing the interactions between White privilege and racism and using White privilege to challenge racism are not original ideas or modern recommendations. As early as 1904, Mary Church Terrell promoted the idea of using White privilege to challenge racist behavior in her essay, "Lynching From a Negro's Point of View" (Jones, 1990). Terrell appealed to Southern White women to use their influence with their fathers, husbands, and sons to abandon the tyranny of lynching (Hurtado, 1996). Her call to use White privilege to oppose racism holds as much relevance today as it did when she first published her essay.

Scholars and social workers like W. E. B. DuBois (1903/1982), Mary Church Terrell (Jones, 1990), and Ida B. Wells-Barnet (Aptheker, 1977) began writing about the structural nature of racism more than one hundred years ago. Given the availability of critical analyses of racism in the United States, contemporary social workers can discover much about their profession and themselves by reflexively interrogating why discourse regarding White privilege is not more prominent in our practice, education, and research. The work to dismantle White privilege involves seeing racism even when it indicts oneself to create a space of relational integrity where all people, those with privilege and those with experiences of oppression, can pool their knowledge and resources to resist manipulation, subjugation, and exploitation.

According to Williams (1988), the NASW and the CSWE established policies designed to combat and eliminate racism within the profession as early as 1969. These efforts have evolved over the last 30 years, and it is NASW's current position that it is "the ethical responsibility of NASW members to assess their own practices and the agencies in which they work for specific ways to end racism where it exists" (Beebe, 1997, p. 264). The CSWE Educational Policy and Accreditation Standards require schools of social work to provide curriculum content that equips students with the skills to promote social change and implement a wide range of interventions that further the achievement of individual and collective social and economic justice (CSWE, 2001).

In spite of these efforts, the social work profession is challenged to consider how traditional approaches might actually perpetuate institutional racism rather than challenge it (Herrick, 1978; McMahon & Allen-Meares, 1992). In 1978 Herrick contended that social work education prepares people for practice in accordance with the prevailing institutional values of our society. Incorporating cultural content about ethnic and racial minorities into a curriculum that supports existing institutional arrangements perpetuates institutional racism (Herrick). Fourteen years later, in 1992, McMahon and Allen-Meares reinforced Herrick's assertion when they maintained that ethnic-sensitive practice, without regard for clients' social and economic contexts, reinforces racist conditions.

Swigonski (1996) suggested that social workers need to work more effectively to transform the social structures that perpetuate racism and all other forms of oppression. A critical element in efforts to eradicate racism and other forms of oppression is identification of the privileges that reproduce injustice. In the past, most of the literature that discussed racism focused on disadvantages and discrimination, ignoring the element of White privilege (Wildman & Davis, 2000). Acknowledging White privilege and developing consciousness of how it is sustained through unquestioned assumptions requires vigilence.

Dalton (1995) advised that even though acknowledging White privilege is difficult, awkward, and discomforting, real progress toward racial healing in the United States depends on it. Racism will persist as long as members of the racially dominant group ignore the benefits that accrue to them from an unjust system of racial stratification (Dalton, 1995; Lipsitz, 1998; McIntosh, 1989; Sleeter, 1996; Wildman, 1996). Discourse regarding White privilege has the potential to inform social workers about a broader view of racism that brings antecedents and consequences into focus. Recognizing the features of White privilege is the first step toward neutralizing its influence. This process requires conscientization, which is developed through the application of critical theories and work in emancipatory movements (Swigonski, 1996).

An antiracist, social work perspective "provides a framework for the critical examination of issues of racism, sexism, classism, anti-Semitism, and heterosexism that are inherent in our society and seeks to bring about social change through collective analysis and action" (James, 1996, p. 8). The ultimate goal of an antiracist approach is to transform the United States into a society of true cultural and racial equality (Wachholz & Mullaly, 2000). Antiracism involves actively working to end racism (Feagin & Vera, 1995; McMahon & Allen-Meares, 1992). Rather than being a new development in social work, the antiracist movement is a return to the approaches espoused during the Settlement House movement and the Civil Rights era (Potocky, 1997).

Social work education is responsible for teaching students about diversity, social justice, racism, sexism, heterosexism, and other forms of oppression (Raske, 1999). Students are encouraged to become culturally competent (Lum, 1999). Pinderhughes (1995) noted that understanding and accepting one's own cultural identity is critical in achieving comfort with the cultural identity of others. Studies about the characteristics of White identity reveal that "Whiteness" is not viewed as identity or a marker for group membership because it is not a problematic characteristic (Hurtado & Stewart, 1997). Failing to understand the meaning of one's own racial identity is a barrier to achieving self-awareness and cultural competence.

Nagda et al. (1999) maintained that the social work classroom can provide a starting point for transformation and justice-oriented practice. Regardless of the approach social work educators use to teach students about the need for societal changes or where this content is located in the curriculum, liberatory education requires a dialectic political analysis that distinguishes the causes and consequences of social problems (Mullaly, 1997). Discourse regarding White privilege is a vital resource for social work education, which is the entrance to the profession. Participant action education is a framework for engaged pedagogy that promotes the type of critical thinking and discourse that challenges White privilege.

References

Adams, M. (1997). Pedagogical frameworks for social justice education. In M. Adams, L. A. Bell, & P. Griffin (Eds.), *Teaching for diversity and social justice: A sourcebook* (pp. 30–43). New York: Routledge.

Adams, M., Blumenfeld, W. J., Castaneda, R., Hackman, H. W., Peters, M. L., & Zuniga, X. (Eds.). (2000). *Readings for diversity and social justice: An anthology on racism, antisemitism, sexism, heterosexism, ableism, and classism.* New York: Routledge.

Aptheker, B. (Ed.). (1977). *Lynching and rape: An exchange of views/by Jane Addams and Ida B. Wells.* New York: American Institute for Marxist Studies.

Bain, K. (2004). *What the best college teachers do.* Cambridge, MA: Harvard University Press.

Beebe, L. (Ed.). (1997). *Social work speaks: NASW policy statements* (4th ed.). Washington, DC: NASW Press.

Bell, L. A. (1997). Theoretical foundations for social justice education. In M. Adams, L. A. Bell, & P. Griffin (Eds.), *Teaching for diversity and social justice: A sourcebook* (pp. 3–15). New York: Routledge.

Boice, R. (2000). *Advice for new faculty members: Nihil nimus.* Needham Heights, MA: Allyn & Bacon.

Christensen, C. P. (1996). The impact of racism on the education of social services workers. In C. E. James (Ed.), *Perspectives on racism in the human services sector: A case for change* (pp. 140–151). Toronto, Canada: University of Toronto Press.

Council on Social Work Education. (2001). *Educational policy and accreditation standards.* Retrieved December 18, 2006, from http://www.cswe.org/

Dalton, H. L. (1995). *Racial healing: Confronting the fear between Blacks and Whites.* New York: Doubleday.

Danielewicz, J. (2001). *Teaching selves: Identity, pedagogy, and teacher education.* Albany: State University of New York Press.

Derman-Sparks, L., & Phillips, C. B. (1997). *Teaching and learning anti-racism: A developmental approach.* New York: Teachers College Press.

Devore, W., & Schlesinger, E. G. (1999). *Ethnic-sensitive social work practice* (5th ed.). Needham Heights, MA: Viacom Company.

Drisko, J. W. (1997). Strengthening qualitative studies and reports: Standards to promote academic integrity. *Journal of Social Work Education, 33,* 185–197.

DuBois, W. E. B. (1982). *The souls of Black folks.* New York: Penguin. (Original work published 1903)

Feagin, J. R., & Vera, H. (1995). *White racism: The basics.* New York: Routledge.

Finlay, L., & Gough, B. (Eds.). (2003). *Reflexivity: A practical guide for researchers in health and social sciences.* Malden, MA: Blackwell Science Ltd.

Flynn, J. (1994). Social justice in social agencies. In R. Edwards (Ed.), *Encyclopedia of social work* (19th ed.) (pp. 2173–2179). Washington, DC: NASW Press.

Fox, H. (2001). *When race breaks out: Conversations about race and racism in college classrooms.* New York: Peter Lang.

Freire, P. (1998). *Pedagogy of freedom: Ethics, democracy, and civic courage* (P. Clarke, Trans.). Lanham, MD: Rowman & Littlefield. (Original work published 1998)

Freire, P. (1997). *Pedagogy of the oppressed* (Rev. ed., M. B. Ramos, Trans.). New York: Continuum. (Original work published 1970)

Germano, W. P. (2005). *From dissertation to book.* Chicago: The University of Chicago Press.

Gould, S. J. (1996). *The mismeasurement of man* (Rev. ed.). New York: Norton.

Green, J. W. (1999). *Cultural awareness in the human services: A multi-ethnic approach* (3rd ed.). Needham Heights, MA: Allyn & Bacon.

Haney Lopez, I. F. (1996). *White by law: The legal construction of race.* New York: New York University Press.

Haney Lopez, I. F. (2000). The social construction of race. In R. Delgado & J. Stefanic (Eds.), *Critical race theory: The cutting edge* (pp. 163–175). Philadelphia: Temple University Press.

Harris, C. I. (1993). Whiteness as property. *Harvard Law Review, 106*(8), 1710–1791.

Healy, K. (2001). Participatory action research and social work: A critical appraisal. *International Social Work, 44*(1), 93–105.

Herrick, J. E. (1978). Perpetuation of institutional racism through ethnic and racial minority content in the curriculum of schools of social work. *Journal of Sociology and Social Welfare, 5*(4), 527–537.

Hilliard, A. G., III. (1998). *SBA: The reawakening of the African mind* (Rev. ed.). Gainesville, FL: Makare Publishing Company.

hooks, b. (1994). *Teaching to transgress: Education as the practice of freedom.* New York: Routledge.

Howard, G. R. (1999). *We can't teach what we don't know: White teachers, multiracial schools.* New York: Teachers College Press.

Hurtado, A. (1996). *The color of privilege: Three blasphemies on race and feminism.* Ann Arbor: University of Michigan Press.

Hurtado, A., & Stewart, A. J. (1997). Through the looking glass: Implications of studying Whiteness for feminist methods. In M. Fine, L. C. Powell, L. Weis, & L. M. Wong (Eds.), *Off white: Readings on society, race, and culture* (pp. 297-311). New York: Routledge.

James, C. E. (Ed.). (1996). *Perspectives on racism and the human services sector: A case for change.* Toronto, Canada: University of Toronto Press.

Jones, B. W. (1990). *Quest for equality: The life and writings of Mary Eliza Church Terrell, 1863–1954.* Brooklyn, NY: Carlson Publishing.

Kemmis, S., & McTaggart, R. (2000). Participatory action research. In N. K. Denzin & Y. S. Lincoln (Eds.), *The handbook of qualitative research* (2nd ed.). Thousand Oaks: CA.

King, J. E. (1991). Dysconscious racism: Ideology, identity, and the miseducation of teachers. *Journal of Negro Education, 60*(2), 133–146.

King, M. L., Jr. (1992). Facing the challenge of a new age. In J. M. Washington (Ed.), *I have a dream: Writings and speeches that changed the world.* New York: HarperCollins.

Kivel, P. (2002). *Uprooting racism: How White people can work for racial justice* (Rev. ed.). Gabriola, B.C., Canada: New Society Publishers.

Lee, J. (1994). *The empowerment approach to social work practice.* New York: Columbia University Press.

Light, R. J. (2001). *Making the most out of college: Students speak their mind.* Cambridge, MA: Harvard University Press.

Lipsitz, G. (1998). *The possessive investment in Whiteness: How White people profit from identity politics.* Philadelphia: Temple University Press.

Lorde, A. (1984). *Sister outsider.* Freedom, CA: The Crossing Press.

Lum, D. (1999). *Culturally competent practice: A framework for growth and action.* Pacific Grove, CA: Brooks/Cole.

Maxwell, J. A. (1996). *Qualitative research design: An interactive approach.* Thousand Oaks, CA: Sage.

McIntosh, P. (1989). White privilege: Unpacking the invisible knapsack. *Peace and Freedom* (July/August), 10–12.

McIntyre, A. (1997). *Making meaning of Whiteness: Exploring racial identity with White teachers.* Albany: State University of New York Press.

McMahon, A., & Allen-Meares, P. (1992). Is social work racist? A content analysis of recent literature. *Social Work, 37*(6), 533–539.

Merriam, S. B. (1998). *Qualitative research and case study applications in education* (Rev. ed.). San Francisco: Jossey-Bass.

Mullaly, R. P. (1997). *Structural social work: Ideology, theory, and practice* (2nd ed.). Ontario, Canada: Oxford University Press.

Nagda, B. A., Spearmon, M. L., Holley, L. C., Harding, S., Balassone, M. L., Moise-Swanson, D., et al. (1999). Intergroup dialogues: An innovative approach to teaching about diversity and justice in social work programs. *Journal of Social Work Education, 35,* 443–449.

National Association of Social Workers. (1999). *Code of ethics of the National Association of Social Workers*. Washington, DC: Author.

Perkinson, H. J. (2002). The critical approach to social work. *Journal of Social Work Education, 38*, 365–368.

Pharr, S. (1996). *In the time of the right: Reflections on liberation*. Berkeley, CA: Chardon Press.

Pinderhughes, E. (1995). Empowering diverse populations: Family practice in the 21st century. *Families in Society: The Journal of Contemporary Human Services, 76*(3), 131–140.

Potocky, M. (1997). Multicultural social work in the United States: A review and critique. *International Social Work, 40*, 315–326.

Rains, F. V. (1998). Is the benign really harmless? Deconstructing some "benign" manifestations of operationalized White privilege. In J. L. Kincheloe, S. R. Steinberg, N. M. Rodriguez, & R. E. Chennault (Eds.), *White reign: Deploying Whiteness in America* (pp. 77–101). New York: St. Martin's Press.

Raske, M. (1999). Using feminist classroom rules to model empowerment to social work students. *Journal of Teaching in Social Work, 19*(1/2), 197–209.

Robbins, S. P., Chatterjee, P., & Canda, E. R. (2006). *Comtemporary human behavior theory: A critical perspective for social work* (2nd ed.). Needham Heights, MA: Allyn & Bacon.

Shor, I., & Freire, P. (1987). *A pedagogy for liberation: Dialogues on transforming education*. South Hadley, MA: Bergin and Garvey Publications.

Sleeter, C. E. (1996). White silence, White solidarity. In N. Ignatiev (Ed.), *Race traitor* (pp. 257–265). New York: Routledge.

Smedley, A. (1993). *Race in North America: Origin and evolution of a worldview*. Boulder, CO: Westview Press.

Swigonski, M. E. (1996). Challenging privilege through Africentric social work practice. *Social Work, 41*(2), 153–161.

Tatum, B. D. (1997). *Why are all the Black kids sitting together in the cafeteria?* New York: Basic Books.

Thandeka. (1999). *Learning to be White: Money, race, and God in America*. New York: Continuum.

Tobach, E., & Rosoff, B. (1994). *Challenging racism and sexism: Alternatives to genetic explanations*. Saline, MI: McNaughton & Gunn.

Vaz, K. M. (1995). Racial aliteracy: White appropriation of Black presences. *Women & Therapy, 16*(4), 31–49.

Wachholz, S., & Mullaly, B. (2000). The politics of the textbook: A content analysis of the coverage and treatment of feminist, radical and anti-racist social work scholarship in American introductory social work textbooks published between 1988 and 1997. *Journal of Progressive Human Services, 11*(2), 51–76.

Weaver, H. N. (2005). *Explorations in cultural competence: Journeys to the four directions*. Belmont, CA: Thomson Brooks/Cole.

Wellman, D. T. (1993). *Portraits of White racism* (2nd ed.). New York: Cambridge University Press.

Wildman, S. M. (1996). *Privilege revealed: How invisible preference undermines America*. New York: New York University Press.

Wildman, S. M., & Davis, A. D. (2000). Language and silence: Making systems of privilege visible. In R. Delgado & J. Stefanic (Eds.), *Critical race theory: The cutting edge* (2nd ed.) (pp. 657–663). Philadelphia: Temple University Press.

Williams, L. F. (1988). Frameworks for introducing racial and ethnic minority content into the curriculum. In C. Jacobs & D. D. Bowles (Eds.), *Ethnicity and race: Critical concepts in social work* (pp. 167–184). Washington, DC: NASW Press.

Williams, P. J. (1997). *Seeing a color-blind future: The paradox of race*. New York: The Noonday Press.

Wolcott, H. F. (1994). *Transforming qualitative data: Description, analysis, and interpretation*. Thousand Oaks, CA: Sage Publications, Inc.

Zinn, H. (1999). *A people's history of the United States: 1492–present* (20th anniversary edition). New York: HarperCollins.

APPENDIX

Targeted Readings

Support for Transformational Critical Consciousness

Delgado, R., & Stefanic, J. (Eds.). (2000). *Critical race theory: The cutting edge* (2nd ed.). Philadelphia: Temple University Press.

Duran, E., & Duran, B. (1995). *Native American post-colonial psychology*. Albany: State University of New York Press.

Frankenberg, R. (1999). *White women, race matters: The social construction of Whiteness*. Minneapolis: University of Minnesota Press.

Freire, P. (1997). *Pedagogy of the oppressed* (Rev. ed., M. B. Ramos, Trans.). New York: Continuum. (Original work published 1970)

Freire, P. (1998). *Pedagogy of freedom: Ethics, democracy, and civic courage* (P. Clarke, Trans.). Lanham, MD: Rowman & Littlefield. (Original work published 1998)

Haney Lopez, I. F. (1996). *White by law: The legal construction of race*. New York: New York University Press.

Helfand, J., & Lippin, L. (2001). *Understanding Whiteness/unraveling racism: Tools for the journey*. Cincinnati, OH: Thomson Learning Custom Publishing.

Helms, J. E. (1992). *A race is a nice thing to have: A guide to being a White person or understanding the White persons in your life*. Topeka, KS: Content Communications.

hooks, b. (1994). *Teaching to transgress: Education as the practice of freedom*. New York: Routledge.

hooks, b. (1995). *Killing rage: Ending racism*. New York: Henry Holt.

hooks, b. (1997). *Wounds of passion: A writing life*. New York: Henry Holt.

Howard, G. R. (1999). *We can't teach what we don't know: White teachers, multiracial schools.* New York: Teachers College Press.

Hurtado, A. (1996). *The color of privilege: Three blasphemies on race and feminism.* Ann Arbor: University of Michigan Press.

Jakobsen, J. R. (1998). *Working alliances and the politics of difference: Diversity and feminist ethics.* Bloomington, IN: Indiana University Press.

Kincheloe, J. L., Steinberg, S. R., Rodriguez, N. M., & Chennault, R. E. (Eds.). (1998). *White reign: Deploying Whiteness in America.* New York: St. Martin's Press.

Kivel, P. (2002). *Uprooting racism: How White people can work for racial justice* (Rev. ed.). Gabriola, B.C., Canada: New Society Publishers.

Lipsitz, G. (1998). *The possessive investment in Whiteness: How White people profit from identity politics.* Philadelphia: Temple University Press.

McIntyre, A. (1997). *Making meaning of Whiteness: Exploring racial identity with White teachers.* Albany: State University of New York Press.

Reddy, M. T. (Ed.). (1996). *Everyday acts against racism: Raising children in a multiracial world.* Seattle, WA: Seal Press.

Tatum, B. D. (1997). *Why are all the Black kids sitting together in the cafeteria?* New York: Basic Books.

Thandeka. (1999). *Learning to be White: Money, race, and God in America.* New York: Continuum.

Zinn, H. (1999). *A people's history of the United States: 1492–present* (20th anniversary edition). New York: HarperCollins.

Sources for Pedagogy Conducive to Participant Action Education

Adams, M., Bell, L. A., & Griffin, P. (Eds.). (1997). *Teaching for diversity and social justice: A sourcebook.* New York: Routledge.

Adams, M., Blumenfeld, W. J., Castaneda, R., Hackman, H. W., Peters, M. L., & Zuniga, X. (Eds.). (2000). *Readings for diversity and social justice: An anthology on racism, antisemitism, sexism, heterosexism, ableism, and classism.* New York: Routledge.

Derman-Sparks, L., & Phillips, C. B. (1997). *Teaching and learning anti-racism: A developmental approach*. New York: Teachers College Press.

Fox, H. (2001). *When race breaks out: Conversations about race and racism in college classrooms*. New York: Peter Lang.

Van Soest, D., & Garcia, B. (2003). *Diversity education for social justice: Mastering teaching skills*. Alexandria, VA: Council on Social Work Education.

INDEX